LIBERATING LEARNING

This book is about three complementary ideas: 1) learning is a practice of freedom; 2) liberating learning in public education requires widespread cultural change in classrooms, schools, and entire education systems; and 3) social movements have been the most powerful vehicles for widespread cultural change, and in their logic of operation lie the keys to liberate learning. Drawing on existing knowledge and new research on educational change, the author offers nine principles of action to liberate learning in schools and across entire educational systems. Topics discussed include learning, pedagogy, leadership, education policy, widespread cultural change, collective action, and whole system improvement. Written for educators and leaders interested in transforming teaching and learning in classrooms and schools, as well as for public intellectuals and people interested in widespread pedagogical change, the book articulates a new way to think about and pursue educational change.

Santiago Rincón Gallardo is an education consultant and chief research officer at Michael Fullan Enterprises.

ROUTLEDGE LEADING CHANGE SERIES

The world is crying out loud for quality education, and for the type of leadership and change to make quality education a reality. Never has there been a greater need for grasping the big pictures of leadership and change in education, which creates the world of tomorrow by developing future generations today.

In this series, you will find some of the world's leading intellectual authorities on educational leadership and change. From the pens of writers such as Dennis Shirley, Pak Tee Ng, Andy Hargreaves, Michael Fullan, Pasi Sahlberg, Alma Harris, Yong Zhao, Amanda Datnow, Vicky Park, Santiago Rincón-Gallardo, Armand Doucet and Karen Edge, come wise insights and breakthrough ideas on this subject. They ask what the new imperatives of educational change are. They explore the paradoxical nature of educational change in celebrated Asian cultures and systems like those of Singapore. They point to the power of professional collaboration and leading from the middle in schools, and networks of schools and across the world, rather than just driving change from the top. They invite us to think about and pursue educational change as social movements aimed at liberating learning. They highlight the surreal nature of leadership and change at this critical moment in world history.

This series of books is for the stout-hearted and open-minded reader who is keenly looking for inspiration to unlock the potential of educational leadership and change in this turbulent world.

Published books in the series include:

Professional Collaboration with Purpose: Teacher Learning Towards Equitable and Excellent Schools
By *Amanda Datnow and Vicki Park*

Surreal Change: The Real Life of Transforming Public Education
By *Michael Fullan*

Learning from Singapore: The Power of Paradoxes
By *Pak Tee Ng*

The New Imperatives of Educational Change: Achievement with Integrity
By *Dennis Shirley*

For more information about this series,
please visit: https://www.routledge.com/
Routledge-Leading-Change-Series/book-series/RLCS.

LIBERATING LEARNING

Educational Change as Social Movement

Santiago Rincón-Gallardo

Routledge
Taylor & Francis Group

NEW YORK AND LONDON

First published 2019
by Routledge
52 Vanderbilt Avenue, New York, NY 10017

and by Routledge
2 Park Square, Milton Park, Abingdon, Oxon OX14 4RN

Routledge is an imprint of the Taylor & Francis Group, an informa business

© 2019 Taylor & Francis

Library of Congress Cataloging-in-Publication Data
A catalog record for this title has been requested

ISBN: 978-1-138-49174-8 (hbk)
ISBN: 978-1-138-49176-2 (pbk)
ISBN: 978-1-351-03210-0 (ebk)

Typeset in Bembo
by Taylor & Francis Books

CONTENTS

PREFACE

Why I Wrote This Book

Through both elementary and high school, I was seen as a highly successful student. Thanks to scholarships, I was privileged to attend a prestigious private school in Mexico City. Each month I proudly brought home a certificate showing I had obtained the highest grades in my group. I represented my school in multiple academic competitions, and often won. In school-wide ceremonies, I often carried the national flag for the full school to sing the national anthem – in Mexico, where I grew up, carrying the national flag is considered one of the highest honours for a student. In essence, I was considered an "excellent" student, one that, according to my teachers, my classmates should emulate.

And yet, when I left high school I didn't really know how to read and write. I could pronounce the words in a text with eloquence, and "finish" entire books. I could even recite entire passages of textbooks shortly after preparing for an exam. But I would have struggled if someone asked me what was the core argument of a story I just read. I would be clueless if asked to identify the strategies used by an author to make a point, let alone articulate my own personal opinion about their ideas. I knew how to put words and sentences together with perfect orthography, impeccable grammar, and beautiful handwriting. Yet I was unable to access my own voice and express it in writing. I took Japanese classes every day for 12 consecutive years. Yet, to this day, I'm unable to maintain a decent conversation with a Japanese speaker for more than 20 seconds. Perhaps more tragically, I left high school practically unable to learn on my own.

Why did I "succeed" at school? I had very good short-term memory. I could memorize entire passages of textbooks the day before an exam and write almost verbatim versions in tests. I became good at understanding and fulfilling the expectations of my teachers. I got especially good at identifying what was required to obtain the best possible grade and doing it. I often ask myself how I could stand to do this for my entire childhood and teenage years. In part my drive may have come from the fact that the early passing of my father – when I was 4 years old and my young sister only 2 – pushed me to feel responsible for helping my mother, who always emphasized the importance of doing well in school. In my world as a child, doing well in school was my most important job. It would make my mother happy and put one less worry on her shoulders. Another reason may be the sense of satisfaction that came from adult approval and the admiration of a good number of my peers. After all, there's something comforting about being liked.

As I entered adolescence, something in my "success" at school started to feel meaningless. I continued to get the highest grades in my class, but I started to rebel. I started to mock some of my teachers when they conveyed incorrect information or when they made requests that felt unreasonable. When I knew it wouldn't affect my grades, I offered evidently absurd responses to questions from my teachers. I got into drawing and doodling to zone out during long and monotonous lectures. I started to cheat in exams. I learned how to make test notes on a translucent sheet, which made it invisible when placed on my dark-wood desk, but allowed me to read it when put on top of a white page. In essence, I figured out how to get the best grades with the least effort and spent the rest of my energy trying to discover all those things that school rules did not forbid and do them. I got a reputation as a troublemaker, but my high grades kept me safe from suspension.

I remember vividly two sour experiences that completed my disillusionment with schooling. In my senior year in middle school, the high school principal saw me at the front desk of the school office. Talking aloud to other teachers in the room while pointing a finger at me, she said: "I'd rather have a student with mediocre grades but good discipline than a guy like this!" This message conveyed to me that the core mission of my school was to discipline us, and that the high grades I had invested so much energy in getting were only secondary to this main purpose.

Later on, in high school, my ethics teacher humiliated a struggling student in front of the whole group and brought her to tears. I stood up and confronted the teacher, calling her out as a bad example of the ethics she was supposed to teach us. I was expelled from the class for the rest of the year. The next day, the high school principal – the same one who had singled me out back in my senior middle school year – came into my classroom and asked me to leave the room. After I left, she warned my peers to stay away from me, that I was a bad influence (a couple of friends told me this afterwards). I was able to maintain some connection with a handful of friends brave enough to defy the principal's instructions. But the overall effect of these events was that I became ostracized by most of my peers.

My experience with schooling offered me two main lessons. One was simulation. Doing well in school was about pretending I was learning while simply getting done the work required to get good grades. But the currency of school grades, which was easy for me to access, was devoid of any intrinsic or lasting value. The second lesson was injustice. It had become clear to me that, in school, obedience and submission took precedence over everything else. My high school graduation was a low point – rather than excitement about the future, my dominant feeling was relief that the pain of school was over.

I went on to the National University of Mexico to start my bachelor's degree in Mathematics. Using basically the same tricks I learned in school, I passed my courses with very decent grades. Mid-way through my college years, the university went on strike. Students, professors, and staff were protesting a proposed legislation that would charge tuition to university students – the National University of Mexico has historically been tuition-free. I had been involved in activism coming out of high school – joining literacy and human rights campaigns in indigenous communities, organizing to support the indigenous Zapatista movement, enrolling volunteers to oversee the first elections of governor in Mexico City. I decided to join the strike. A series of events led the most aggressive and intolerant sector of the movement to take control. Ultimately, I and other colleagues who had been organizing forums to discuss the future of public university in Mexico, were expelled from the strike.

It was at that time that my life took an unexpected and fortunate turn. Gabriel Cámara – one of the most important living education thinkers and doers in Latin America – was looking for someone to join his team to design and run an education programme for small, rural communities across the country. He contacted me by recommendation of a university professor who taught a seminar on math education that I had taken. With my school on strike and eager to start a formal job, I accepted Gabriel's invitation. The programme, called "Post-primary Project", was housed by the National Council for the Promotion of Education (CONAFE, for its initials in Spanish), the branch of the Mexican Ministry of Education that provides educational services to small, scattered rural communities across the country.

The Post-primary Project aimed at encouraging young people and adults living in the most remote communities to learn independently from written sources. Grounded on the fundamental axiom that meaningful learning occurs when the interest of a learner meets the capacity of an educator to support them, in Post-primary centres each student could choose a topic of study and receive tutorial support from a tutor. Independent learning took centre stage and, from the outset, the Post-primary Project ignored standard teaching; there were no fixed programmes, syllabi, or certifying systems. Subject matter was but an excuse to develop more durable intellectual habits.

Gabriel's educational philosophy and practice had been influenced by the ideas of his close friends Paulo Freire and Ivan Illich, two of the most prominent education thinkers of the 1970s. He saw in literacy an enormous potential for individual and collective liberation. The Post-primary Project offered an opportunity to test ideas that until then had only been tried out on a small scale.

One of Gabriel's most important decisions with the Post-primary Project was to keep design and execution tightly linked. In practice, this meant that the leaders of the project at the national level had to demonstrate that their ideas could work in practice. Our team spent a lot of time in Post-primary centres, not to evaluate teachers and their practice, but to assess our own model, test our assumptions, and adapt to ensure the pedagogical practice we envisioned became a reality.

Our constant review and adaptation of the Post-primary training model revealed a fundamental contradiction between the training we were delivering and the practice that we expected to see in classrooms. The national team included specialists in different academic subjects, with each specialist responsible for training Post-primary educators in that area of expertise. The mathematician led the math training, the literacy expert led the literacy training, and so on. Our expectation, however, had been that young instructors working day to day in Post-primary centres would support the independent learning of their students across all subject matters. But this was not occurring.

The revelation of this core contradiction led us to redefine our training model. If we wanted instructors to be able to support the independent learning of topics across subjects, we had to demonstrate first that we were able to do it ourselves. We decided to become a learning community. The mathematician started to dive into poetry and short stories with the support of the literature specialist, the English specialist started to tackle math problems with the support of the mathematician, and so on. Each of us was expected to demonstrate our learning in public. The national team of the Post-primary Project became a learning community, a living example of the pedagogy that we expected to see in schools. This became a core feature of our work, which later on took on different names – first the Learning Community Project, more recently Tutorial Networks.

This experience changed my life. With the support of expert colleagues, I learned to make meaning and experience the beauty of initially obscure poems; I dived deep into novels that I had "read" many times in the past but, for the first time, I was able to engage in sustained conversation with the authors and discover the strategies they used to surprise me, to make me feel moved, and so on. I experienced thinking like a scientist when exploring puzzling questions such as "how was John Dalton able to demonstrate that atoms exist when there were no microscopes powerful enough to see them?" or "how do airplanes fly?"; I experienced thinking like a historian when I read original works about the Conquest of Mexico and the Mexican Revolution, and explored how the authors were able to articulate their theories of why and how things happened, in spite of having no direct access to people who lived at the time.

For the first time, I experienced the joy of making sense of questions that puzzled me, using written text as the medium. I felt the joy of finding meaning in initially obscure texts after persisting through the struggle of learning deeply. I became confident that I could learn whatever I set myself to learn – not superficially to get a good grade, but with deep understanding. With this experience, I also found my voice. I started to write almost compulsively about what and how I was learning, both as a student myself, and as an education leader trying to figure out ways to enable others to learn autonomously. Over the four years I worked with the Post-primary team, I co-authored two books.

What I learned those days has stayed in my flesh and heart. When the university strike resumed, I decided to continue working with Gabriel full-time instead of going back to school. I managed to convince teachers of the courses I had to pass to complete my Bachelor's degree to let me enrol in their course, skip classes, and write final exams at the end of the semester. Using my newly acquired skills and confidence to learn independently, I dove into the core books for courses on mathematical analysis, theory of numbers, projective geometry, game theory, and the like. I made a habit of solving all the problems at the end of each chapter, including the most challenging ones.

Without access to information on the expectations of the teacher, I became my own and most rigorous teacher. I got straight "A"s in the final exams. This time around, however, the "A"s had behind them the deep satisfaction that comes from gaining mastery of and knowing the subject in depth. Ironically, I learned Math best when I stopped attending classes. Writing my thesis was relatively easy, although combining a full-time job with completing my university credits led me to graduate ten years after enrolling. I got my Bachelor's diploma the same day I received an acceptance letter from Harvard to a Master's programme on International Education Policy. I moved to Boston in 2006 to begin the programme, never before having used English to communicate orally or in writing (yes, there was some cheating here, too: I got a lot of help to write my statement of purpose from bilingual friends). Once again, it was the confidence in my own capacity to learn acquired during my years working with Gabriel Cámara that helped me navigate life and take graduate courses in a second language, and to gain pretty decent mastery of English in a relatively short period of time.

I continue to learn to this day. And this is one of the most precious gifts life has given me. After all, learning is, at its core, a practice of freedom. But the deep influence of my years working alongside Gabriel Cámara and my comrades in Mexico goes well beyond my own personal growth. Perhaps more importantly, it comes from witnessing the transformative power that the experience of learning in depth has in others – children, youth, and adults alike. The work of Gabriel and his team (many of them former leaders of the Post-primary Project) to foster and spread pedagogies and environments that nurture the skills and habits of independent learning has gone through several iterations. Over and over again, I have seen the tremendous power that deep learning has to change individual lives, communities, and the world. The spark in the eyes of children and adults when they figure out a solution to a question they've been tackling for days, their renewed sense of confidence and joy in learning, their uncontainable impulse to help others learn what they themselves have learned well, continue to inspire my thinking and my work in education to this day.

My frustrating experience in school and the contrasting, liberating experience of learning deeply outside of school have shaped me in profound ways. I have dedicated my professional life to understanding how and under what conditions powerful pedagogies can spread at scale. Behind this intellectual pursuit lies a larger purpose, inspired by the desire that every human being experiences the liberation that comes from learning deeply – and that they are freed from the dehumanizing and dreadful effects of conventional schooling. Through my interactions with thousands of students, teachers, educational administrators, and friends over the past two decades, I have learned that my story is the story of many who have attended school. The details will vary widely, but the sense of dislocation between schooling and powerful learning might be, in this era, an almost universal human experience.

I am convinced that powerful learning is within the reach of anyone, and that the strategies to make it happen are relatively simple. I strongly believe that schools – for the most part unintentionally – do more harm than good when it comes to nurturing the mindsets required to learn deeply and, more broadly, to nurture vibrant, robust democracies. I am also aware that conventional schooling is one of the most resilient institutions ever created by humans, and that it won't disappear into oblivion without a big fight. I remain convinced, however, that within each of us lies the most powerful, and still untapped, resource to turn schools and entire school systems into places for powerful learning. This resource, the resource most equally distributed among us humans, is our capacity to act, learn, and change the world. I've seen it work, and I trust we'll see it work more and more in the coming years.

ACKNOWLEDGEMENTS

More people than I would be able to mention in a few pages have influenced the thinking behind and the completion of this book. Knowledge is always a collective endeavour, and many of the ideas we may consider our own have been expressed in one way or another by someone else, elsewhere, at some other time. Here I mention the people and groups to whom I attribute the most direct and prominent influence in the conceptualization, revision, and execution of this work. However, my gratefulness extends also to those unintentionally omitted. It is on the shoulders of giants, some explicitly named, others implicitly evoked, that I have had an opportunity to stand. While the people and groups listed here have influenced this book in very important ways, I take full responsibility for the interpretations I make of their ideas.

The seminal source of the ideas I've developed on educational change is to be found in the change leaders and practitioners whom I've had the privilege to interact with over the past two decades and who, through their work and audacious leadership, have built bastions of hope for the future of educational change, both in the Global South and in North America. These include: CONAFE and Redes de Tutoría in México; Escuela Nueva in Colombia; Educación 2020 in Chile; the California Department of Education; the Twin Rivers Unified School District, the Garden Grove Unified School District, the Whittier Union High School District, the Corona Norco Unified School District, the Fresno Unified School District, and the Long Beach Unified School District in California; the Ontario Ministry of Education; the Ottawa Catholic School Board, the Simcoe County District School Board; and the Algoma District School Board in Ontario; and the Institute for Democratic Education in America.

Gabriel Cámara, my mentor, Dalila López, and my colleagues in Redes de Tutoría, S.C. shaped in fundamental ways my educational philosophy. It is from and with them that I learned that the educational world is best understood when you deliberately try to transform it, and that how much we can expect others to change is a function to how much we are willing and able to change ourselves.

Richard Elmore was the first to qualify our work of widespread pedagogical change in Mexico as a social movement, after his visit to the country in 2010. This insight provoked in me something that I can only describe as an intellectual awakening. It crystalized and integrated in my mind several ideas that had until then felt scattered, disorganized, and unclear. Since then, Richard Elmore has been incredibly kind and generous to spare time to help us think more deeply about the implications of this work in Mexico and beyond.

Marshall Ganz offered key ideas and resources for the ideas presented here. He brought to my attention *Culture Moves*, by Thomas Rochon, which examines how and under what conditions widespread cultural change occurred over a 150-year-span of American history. This work, as well as his own scholarship on social movements and leadership, became major influences in the theoretical framing of the ideas presented here.

Michael Fullan appeared as a blessing in my life, at a time when I was about to complete my doctoral studies at Harvard, about to become a first-time father, and looking for a decent job in Toronto, where I was a newcomer. I couldn't have asked for a more ideal mentor. Over the past six years I've had the privilege to work alongside him conducting research and supporting educational system leaders in designing and developing strategies to improve teaching and learning across entire provinces and States, both in North and South America. Working alongside him has afforded me the best possible intensive learning on educational change, strategic thinking, and speed writing (I aspire to get to the point of writing three books a year, like he's done since I met him). Many of the ideas from the educational change turf presented here, as well as the writing style of the book have more than a touch of Michael's indelible influence.

Andy Hargreaves has shown an interest and faith in my work that sometimes feels unwarranted. His invitation to write a book for the Leading Change Series alongside giants in the field is an incommensurable honour. His availability to discuss the ideas on this book all the way from its very inception to its publication, and his thoughtful and helpful support as editor throughout the whole process, have made this book much better than it would have been otherwise.

Over the past six years I've had the privilege of meeting and developing friendships with powerful thinkers of the educational change field, including Andy Hargreaves and Dennis Shirley at Boston College, Beatriz Point at the OECD, Carol Campbell, Nina Bascia, Steve Anderson, and Rubén Gaztambide-Fernández at the Ontario Institute for Studies in Education, Joelle Rodway at Memorial University in Newfoundland, Tricia Niesz at Kent University, Viviane Robinson at New Zealand's University of Auckland, Vicky Colbert of Colombia's Escuela Nueva, Brahm Fleisch of South Africa's Gauteng Literacy and Mathematics Strategy, Rukmini Banerji of India's Pratham, and many more. The ideas in this book would not have been possible without the multiple conversations and discussions in their offices, over Skype, over lunch, in courses, seminars, and conferences.

Nancy Watson kindly agreed to review and edit the almost final version of my manuscript. Thanks to her thorough, candid, and on-point editing, this book is now much clearer and in much better shape than what I could have accomplished on my own.

My wife Asha, and our beloved 6- and 2-year-old boys, Kai and Koji, have most heavily felt the countless hours I spent reading, writing, and thinking aloud and in silence to complete this book. Investing time into this work meant taking away invaluable time from our family activities, and my gratefulness for their patience and support can only be measured, if at all, through transfinite arithmetic.

Much of the original research that helped shape the ideas presented in this book was supported by a generous Banting Post-doctoral Fellowship, which I held at the Ontario Institute for Studies in Education, University of Toronto between 2014 and 2016; grants from the *Consejo Nacional de Ciencia y Tecnología* and *Fundación México en Harvard, A.C.*; and professional and financial support from Michael Fullan Enterprises, Inc.

1

INTRODUCTION

For a few centuries [sapiens] has tried to make himself like a machine
[S]He's learned to arrive on time.
[S]He's learned to repeat after teacher.
[S]He's learned to do repetitious tasks reliably.
Machines are now better at being machines than [sapiens] is.
[Sapiens] must now relearn how to be [hu]man

Tweet by @TheStoicEmperor

Ideas are powerful forces. They shape not only how we think about the world but, perhaps most importantly, how we act on it. Our ways of thinking about the world delimit what we believe is possible and desirable – what we can and should do. One set of ideas in particular has shaped in deep and pervasive ways how we have acted in our schools and educational systems for over a century. This set of ideas is *scientific management*, a way of thinking and acting that emerged in the wake of the industrial revolution in the early twentieth century. In an era where mass production and efficiency were considered key forces for economic growth and prosperity, scientific management was a revolutionary idea. It proposed that the best way to organize human activity was to break down complex work into small, repetitive and routine tasks, with external incentives to ensure adequate execution of the work. Mass compulsory schooling was an invention that responded to the needs of the industrial revolution, which resulted in waves of immigration from the countryside to cities for work in emerging industries. We needed a place to send our kids while adults were working. We needed a way to ensure a somewhat harmonious social order and prevent the chaos that the arrival, fast and *en masse*, of new people to the cities could bring. And the new industrial order required mechanisms to sort and select the future managers.

Schools and school systems, along with many other organizations, were profoundly shaped by the ideas of scientific management. Organizing students by age, breaking down the day in timed blocks with each group following instructions from the adult in the room, and creating external incentives such as grades became, and indeed continue to be, some of their key defining features of schools and school systems. This was an effective way to manage large numbers of students.

The problem is that, *learning* – at least joyful, self-directed learning – was set aside. Scientific management assumed that work was inherently boring and meaningless – and thus the importance of creating external incentives for its execution. And in many ways, this is what school work has become – a series of tasks to get done for compliance, good grades, and certificates.

Few experiences are as liberating, joyful and intrinsically motivating as powerful learning. Making sense of questions that matter to us is inherent to our human condition. Seeing the spark in the eyes of children and youth when they figure out solutions to problems that matter to them is one of the most powerful sources of meaning for educators and administrators alike.

This book is about three complementary ideas:

- Powerful learning is liberating for those who experience it;
- Classrooms, schools, and entire educational systems can be transformed in the service of liberating learning; and
- This can be best achieved through social movements organized around liberating learning.

Imagine that we stopped thinking for a moment about formal education as a technical solution to managing large groups of students efficiently. Imagine we thought instead of education as a vehicle to ignite the innate capacity of every human being to learn and change the world. And that we used this as our starting point to create practices and strategies to liberate learning in schools and across entire educational systems. This book is my invitation to reimagine how we think about and pursue educational change.

Reimagining Educational Change

I will start with the pessimistic part. I promise optimism awaits a couple pages ahead. As a father of two young boys, and as a human, I am deeply worried about the state of the world. Many rapidly unfolding trends and conditions are forcing us to rethink, individually and collectively, what we stand for and what we want to become. Such worrisome changes include, among many others: the rapidly growing scale and speed of natural disasters caused by human activity; the prospects of extinction of life on the planet; mass global migration and displacement; and the rise of fundamentalism and violence.

In this daunting scenario, it is worth asking ourselves what schools and school systems can and should do to give our children a fighting chance to survive, thrive in, and positively change a highly unpredictable and unjust world. Schools already face unreasonable expectations concerning problems in society. But education for the future is not about adding more to the pile of things teachers and school leaders are expected to do. It is about pausing to redefine our key priorities, and then learning to do things differently.

What legacy can public education give to our young people to give them a fighting chance to survive and thrive? Learning to learn deeply is top of my list. If our kids will have to solve problems that are bigger and more complex than those we know how to solve, the best we can do for them is nurture their ability to learn on their own, to find joy in their power to learn, and to make the world a better place. The current legacy of schooling, at best, falls short and, at worst, is disabling our younger generations for the future. High school diplomas, university degrees, grades and standardized test scores, among other measures of attainment, may have worked as predictors of individual success (income, employment, physical and mental health) and some measures of social wellbeing (economic development, safety). But they tell us little about the extent to which young people are prepared to learn whatever they will have to learn to address the massive challenges ahead. They tell us little about whether they are prepared to pursue individual and collective freedom, build robust democracies, and contribute to sustaining life on the planet. Schools as we know them are far from preparing our young people for what's coming and, in many ways, for what's already here. Reimagining classrooms, schools, and educational systems so that they become vibrant places for learning and living examples of the societies we aspire to become is more urgent than ever. It is indeed crucial for our survival.

Reinventing schools and school systems requires also that we reimagine educational change. By "educational change" I mean the body of knowledge and ideas that has developed as an attempt to better understand and improve efforts to reform schools and school systems. Over several decades, the educational change field has offered robust findings that continue to be relevant in the pursuit of radically new versions of schools and school systems. At the same time, the future of educational change requires that we look directly at two blindspots: learning and power. And when these two are brought front and centre, we are compelled to shift how we understand and pursue educational change.

Overall, the educational change field has assumed that formal education – or schooling – is inherently good, directly and unquestionably linked to human progress and wellbeing. But a different picture emerges when we dare to look directly at its key blind spots. Let's start with learning.

Where Did Learning Go?

Ironically, student learning has remained a marginal area of concern for the educational change field. A historical review of the *Journal of Educational Change*, for example, reported that student learning has been seriously overlooked over the 15-year span of the journal's existence (García-Huidobro, Nannemann, Bacon, & Thompson, 2017). With a widely shared focus on understanding and fostering large-scale, sustainable school improvement through the professionalism of educators, only a marginal number of articles touch directly upon student learning. Furthermore, when student learning is given some attention, it is through proxies, most prominently student achievement scores, course completion, graduation rates, and the like.[1]

In the educational change field, learning has been primarily valued for its functional value – for example, scores in standardized testing as indicators of knowledge and skills for future employability, and high-school certificates as standardized measures of college or career readiness. Learning is rarely seen as an intrinsic value, a liberating act, a deliberate practice with larger societal implications.

Compulsory school systems were not originally designed to foster learning – certainly not finding creative solutions to problems, communicating effectively, collaborating with others or deliberately transforming the world for the better. The historical role of schools has been custody, control, and sorting. With the waves of immigration that started to pour into big cities after the industrial revolution at the end of the nineteenth century and the wake of the twentieth century, governments had to find ways to provide custody to children, to shape the future work force (mostly low-skilled factory workers), and to identify the selected few who would access managerial roles. Schooling emerged and stuck as the preferred solution. The design of schooling, as with many organizations and companies of the time, found inspiration in the scientific management principles of Fredrick Taylor: activities broken down into simple, repetitive tasks carried out by low-skilled workers, and external incentives (punishments and rewards) to ensure tasks were completed. These principles continue to influence how many organizations, schools included, operate to this day. Indeed, the fundamental design of schooling has remained practically unchanged more than a century later.

To be sure, throughout this period, more powerful ideas about learning have shaped the discourse around the desirability and virtues of schools. Progressive educators and thinkers such as John Dewey and Maria Montessori offered powerful insights into the nature of learning. But while ideas of this sort have continued to exist throughout the history of compulsory schooling, they rarely influenced more than a small proportion of educators and schools. Instead, schools came to resemble factories or prisons more than they did vibrant environments for learning.

Of course, many of us have fond memories of school. Many of us remember one or two teachers who touched our lives and changed their course for the better. There is immense value in having institutions that offer a relatively safe and stable environment to children while parents are working.[2] There is value in having spaces where children can socialize and learn to live with others. But when it comes to learning – what specifically do we take away from school and how much of it do we actually remember or use? – the balance is less encouraging.

Not only were schools not designed to foster learning; they can *get in the way* of learning. They do this, sometimes unintentionally, other times deliberately, through prioritizing compliance, compartmentalizing knowledge, creating fear of failure, and concentrating control in the hands of adults. Critics of schooling have pointed out such effects for decades. In 1970 Ivan Illich, in his classic *Deschooling Society*, argued and predicted that, after reaching a certain scale, institutions would start to direct their functions towards their own perpetuation, moving away from, and even working against, the purposes for which they were built: medical institutions creating widespread disease (currently medical error is among the top three causes of death in the United States, together with heart disease and cancer);[3] super highways creating massive traffic congestions; schools preventing learning. A few years later, John Holt (1977), a passionate educator and an eloquent critic of schooling, poignantly said that if schools were responsible to teach kids to talk, the world would be full of mute people and stutterers. In the early 1990s, New York State Teacher of the Year, John Taylor Gatto, announced in an op-ed piece in the *Wall Street Journal* his decision to quit teaching because he was no longer willing to hurt children. A decade ago, Kirsten Olson (2009) set out to interview a whole range of highly accomplished professionals in search for their most powerful learning experiences in school. Instead, the consistent theme she found across the narratives is captured in the title of her bestselling book: *Wounded by School*. Highly accomplished professionals succeeded despite, rather than thanks to, school. Sir Ken Robinson, in his highly popular TED talk, has eloquently articulated how schools crush the natural creativity and curiosity of children. More recently, Tony Wagner and Ted Dintersmith, in their book *Most Likely to Succeed* (Wagner & Dintersmith, 2015), argue that what schools are teaching kids is for the most part irrelevant. And the list goes on.

Schooling has historically faced a core contradiction, which has become more blatantly evident, and increasingly unbearable over time: being the institutions charged with educating our younger generations, they are not only failing to nurture and develop their abilities to learn, but also crushing their ability and their joy to do it. Evidence of this core contradiction abounds. A simple test, called the Torrance Test for Creative Thinking, has been used to measure the capacity to think creatively, starting with young kindergarten children and tracking their creativity over time (Kim, 2011; Torrance, 1968). These studies consistently find that creative thinking declines sharply as children go through school. As reported by Mirjam Schöning and Christina Witcomb (2017) from the LEGO Foundation in a blog post for the World Economic Forum, while 98 per cent of children in kindergarten score in the "creative genius" category, their creative ability is drastically diminished as they grow older (Schöning & Witcomb, 2017). By age 25, only 3 per cent remain creative geniuses. Children's enthusiasm with school also goes through remarkable decline over time (Lepper, Corpus, & Iyengar, 2005). As an illustration, in 2012, Lee Jenkins, former district superintendent, asked about 2,000 of the elementary and secondary school teachers in his seminars to indicate the grade level they were teaching and the percentage of students in that grade whom they believed loved school. While teachers in kindergarten reported that, on average, 95 per cent of their children loved school, the average percentage reported by teachers in grade 9 was 37 per cent (Jenkins, 2012).[4]

Recent discoveries on the psychology of motivation and the neuroscience of learning are making the core contradiction of schooling even more evident. It is now a well-established finding that the following four conditions drive intrinsic motivation: purpose, autonomy, mastery, and connectedness. Learning and doing things that matter to us (purpose), with freedom to decide what, how, when, and with whom to do it (autonomy), getting better over time (mastery), and doing it with others (connectedness), are the core conditions needed to do what we do with full intention and focus. Yet all four conditions are rather absent in most schools and classrooms around the world. Indeed, the four opposite conditions offer a more accurate description of conventional schooling: little to no intrinsic purpose; control by adults over what, how, when, and with whom to "learn"; emphasis on "covering" as much content as possible; individualism and competition.

Neuroscience is making breakthrough discoveries about our natural inclination and our biological need to learn, as well as the conditions that nurture or inhibit such inclination.[5] We know, for example, that in the act of learning our brains release dopamine, a hormone that produces feelings of pleasure and fulfilment. Learning always involves encountering something we don't fully understand or cannot initially do, and our brains thrive on situations where we are faced with problems situated in what Lev Vygotsky (1978) called the *zone of proximal development*: the bordering zone in between what we know and are able to do and what we don't yet know or aren't able to do. The sense of feeling close to a new understanding or solution but not yet knowing whether we will succeed produces excitement and pleasure. Our brains not only *can* learn: they *need to* learn.

The brain learns by developing increasingly dense networks of neurons, and by pruning and reorganizing existing networks into more efficient forms of cognitive and affective processing. Language as the means of making sense of the world is the main vehicle through which this happens. It is through constant exposure and use of language and meaning-making that our brains create and solidify structures for future use in thinking and creating. This process of neuronal network development reaches its highest peak in adolescence.

Now, in order for our brains to make the neuronal connections that make learning possible, the learner needs to feel safe to take risks and fail, whereas fear shuts down the possibility of those neuronal connections, activating instead our amygdala to send our brains a signal to fight or flight for our survival. Furthermore, the brain responds to boredom almost identically to how it responds to threat: Boredom activates the amygdala, releasing the same stress hormones that create the fight or flight response. Putting a person in a situation of chronically low stimulation and affective and cognitive disengagement creates the same withdrawal and avoidance response as an external threat.[6] Seen from this perspective, conventional schooling starts to look like a less-than-ideal, if not toxic, environment for learning: The need for certainty and predictability, the fear to fail and make mistakes, and boredom are a rather constant part of the everyday experiences of millions of children and youth in classrooms around the world.

A first order of business for the future of educational change is to zero in on learning. And, more specifically, on deep learning, which I define as the process and the result of making sense of questions that matter to us. Its associated competencies are critical thinking, creativity, collaboration, communication, compassion, and character (Fullan, Quinn, & McEachen, 2017). Deep learning can nurture in our young people the skills and habits of mind that will be required to solve the current and future problems faced by humanity and the planet. What do classrooms, schools, and entire school systems look like when deep learning is their primary purpose? What does it take to adapt schooling to the learning of our students, as opposed to forcibly trying to adapt the learning of our students to the logic of schooling? How can adults learn to fundamentally transform classroom, school, and system practices so that they liberate learning? How can education systems reorganize themselves to focus deliberately on liberating learning? There are emerging examples that offer glimpses into what classrooms schools, and systems of this kind might look like, as well as emerging clarity about how to go about liberating learning at scale. I will touch upon these throughout the book. For now, let me shed light on the second blind spot of educational change: power.

And Democracy? And Freedom?

The basic unit where learning happens or not is the pedagogical core[7] – that is, the relationship between an educator and a learner in the presence of knowledge (Cohen, Ball, Raudenbush, & Ball, 2003; Hawkins, 1974). As Walter Doyle (1983) puts it, what students learn is a direct function of the tasks they are asked to do. Over the past decade or so, the educational change field has seen a growing interest in changing the pedagogical core on the grounds that doing so is the most direct pathway to improved student learning.[8]

There is another reason why changing the pedagogical core is important, with key implications for democracy and the pursuit of individual and collective freedom. As much as it is the basic unit of learning, the pedagogical core is also a basic unit of dominant relationships of power and authority. To this day, the dominant pattern of relationships within the pedagogical core is hierarchical in nature, with clear divisions of power and control. Broadly speaking, knowledge (or the curriculum) presides over teachers, and teachers preside over students. There is a clear vertical division between who determines what is to be done and who is expected to follow the instructions of the one above. Looked at from this perspective, conventional schooling is not only a disservice to learning, but also to democracy.

Our classrooms and schools should be an example of the societies we aspire to become. Inspired in their original design by the principles of scientific management, however, schools have historically looked and continue to look more like factories or prisons than like vibrant places for learning and democracy building: Groups of children sent to an institution they have not chosen to attend; organized by age; moving through pre-determined blocks of time under the direction of an adult who dictates what is to be done, when, and how; expected to sit quietly and listen attentively to and follow the instructions of the adult; constantly exposed to a system of extrinsic motivators to do their work (grades, golden stars, adult approval).

Indeed, the first compulsory schooling system in the world, which inspired the "one-best system" of schooling in the United States (Tyack, 1974), and later on across the Americas and the world, was created in Prussia, under the totalitarian regime of Frederick the Great (Gatto, 2009; van Horn Melton, 2003). At the time, compulsory schooling was intentionally devised as a vehicle to control and homogenize the younger generations, to shape a predictable citizenry and an easily manageable workforce.[9] While current education discourse, plans, and policies will hardly portray formal schooling as a vehicle for control, the way it functions ends up fulfilling this role very well.

In *Dumbing Us Down: The Hidden Curriculum of American Schools*, John Taylor Gatto (1992) argues that schools teach children seven key lessons: confusion, class position, indifference, emotional and intellectual dependency, conditional self-esteem, and surveillance. These seven lessons are contrary to and seriously undermine democracy, as well as individual and collective freedom. They are more fitting to totalitarian regimes than to robust democracies.

I prefer to think that today's schools and school systems function the way they do more because of habit and inertia than because of a deliberate intention to keep people ignorant, acritical, and subdued. But some argue that school systems continue to exist precisely because they work successfully in the service of big corporate and authoritarian interests: passive consumerism feeding the economy; acritical, misinformed, and fearful masses tolerating abusive and blatantly unjust policies, et cetera. And they have a point. In any case, the answer will become clearer once movements to substantially redefine public schooling start to become more prominent. Will these movements be able to advance their cause with little resistance from political elites and big corporations? Will they be proactively attacked, and if so, by whom and why? In any case, the best way to figure out will be to do the work of transforming schools and school systems into vibrant places for learning and examples of the societies we aspire to become, while keeping an eye on the reactions from the institutional, political, and social environments where schooling is embedded.

Interestingly, the skillsets and mindsets required for powerful learning are starting to converge with those required for employability and for the creation of robust democracies. Productive economies, sustainable ecosystems, and vibrant democracies now require people who can think critically, find creative solutions to complex problems, communicate effectively, collaborate with others, act with compassion and solidarity, and self-regulate. For this reason, deep learning has the potential to bridge educational change and social justice, two fields that have so far evolved separately from each other. Let's unpack this argument a bit.

Freire Meets Dewey[10]

I am often surprised by the clear, almost visible schism that seems to exist between those interested in educational change and those invested in social justice. A first way one can make this split visible, albeit imperfectly, is along racial lines. Walk into an educational research conference session or take a quick pick on a list of the most prominent authors on educational change and you will most likely see a majority of white people. At a social justice session in the same conference, or upon reviewing a list of social justice authors, people of colour will most likely be the majority, or at least appear in larger proportions. If you listen carefully to the ideas discussed in these two worlds, you will identify differences in key concepts, concerns, and epistemological stances. Prominent topics in the educational change field will include instructional improvement, the teaching profession, student achievement, policy implementation, organizational leadership, and whole system reform. In the social justice camp, prominent concerns will include teacher and youth activism, community and political organizing, and the oppressive nature of schooling.

The distinction just outlined is less clear-cut and more imperfect than portrayed. To be sure, there is educational change work that touches upon issues of social justice – most prominently work concerned with reporting achievement gaps, describing "unexpected" schools and systems that succeed "against the odds" of having high proportions of students of colour and in poverty[11] and, more recently, work that suggests that better quality in educational services can – and should – be pursued through increased equity.[12] But educational change has treated social justice rather superficially in at least two crucial ways. First, issues of power and liberation remain either marginal or altogether invisible in the educational change field. Second, the connection between schools and the context surrounding them rarely takes centre stage.

With its focus on issues of power and equity, the social justice field has advanced knowledge and action around these two areas, which have been left mostly unexamined within the educational change field. Now, just as the social justice field points to some of the key blind spots of the educational change field, the educational change field has advanced knowledge on areas that have been mostly overlooked in the social justice field, such as change leadership, change knowledge, and whole system change. It seems obvious that both fields (educational change and social justice) will greatly benefit from listening to and learning from each other. Yet the links between both so far have been weak. Pedagogy, with its dual and direct link to learning and power, offers a rich seam for educational change and social justice to connect and strengthen each other.

Now, the pedagogical realm has also been split in siloes, along the same lines that educational change and social justice have evolved separately from each other. Sarah Fine (2017) has called this the Dewey–Freire divide.[13] On the Dewey side lie so called progressive educators – mostly white people – who have explored and pursued learning as the natural inclination of children. Progressive educators have been mostly concerned with themes and questions that have been pursued through traditional academic disciplines – mathematics, science, history, et cetera. In this sense, constructivist methodologies have been best suited to the development of disciplined academic thinking and problem solving, which in turn has been historically valued as an entry ticket to higher education and employment.

On the Freire side is the field of critical pedagogy – with a much wider representation of people of colour – which sees and pursues education as a means for people (young people as well as adults) to gain awareness of their oppressive conditions and take emancipatory action. With its emphasis on examining and dismantling some of the most blatant and evident forms of oppression, critical pedagogy has been best suited to the pursuit of social justice and robust democracy.

We are living in a world where both the pursuit of social justice and the ability to understand and solve complex problems are equally urgent. No doubt young people – and the adults they look up to for guidance – have to understand and dismantle deeply embedded forms of oppression such as racism, sexism, misogyny, xenophobia, and the like. But they also have to be prepared to tackle massive and complex problems such as those posed by the predicted disappearance of most jobs in the next few decades, the rise of fundamentalism and violence, not to mention climate change and the prospects of the extinction of life on the planet. And we can no longer afford to prioritize one set of problems over the other. As I mentioned earlier, the emerging concept of deep learning has the potential to tend a bridge between critical pedagogy and constructivist pedagogies. This is so because the skillsets and mindsets required for robust democracies are starting to converge with those required for problem solving and employability.

So far, the Dewey–Freire divide has kept two powerful sets of ideas and practices ignoring or fighting each other, while both remain either marginal or fully neglected in the larger educational change field. And, perhaps more importantly, while these two siloes continue to ignore or fight each other, a greater enemy continues unabated: the default culture of schooling. The question is not whether constructivist pedagogies are more important or relevant than critical pedagogies. The question is: Why haven't either taken root and spread beyond a minimal set of classrooms or schools? Constructivist and critical pedagogies pop up here and there in a handful of classrooms and schools through the extraordinary efforts of a few extraordinary educators, but the dominant logic of schooling remains unchanged.

Freire and Dewey need each other because both sets of ideas have failed to take hold in the vast majority of schools across entire educational systems. As revolutionary thinker Antonio Gramsci would put it, they have both failed to establish a new hegemony – that is, a set of ideas, beliefs, and practices that are widely shared in a social group and become the new taken-for-granted. They have fallen short of subverting and redefining the institutional culture and power relationships of schooling, which gets as much in the way of learning (a core concern for Dewey) as in the way of social justice and democracy (a core concern for Freire).

I have recently articulated four theses that may help us get Freire and Dewey to listen to and learn from each other while walking towards the future (Rincón-Gallardo, 2018). These theses constitute a basic set of propositions, grounded on evidence, that underlie the core ideas developed throughout the book.

Learning Is a Practice of Freedom

Whatever its *content* (be it understanding a mathematical principle, making sense of a poem, or examining what gets on the way of fairness in a school), learning is, at its core, a liberating act. It involves getting immersed in and making sense of questions that matter to us, with autonomy to decide on the pace and form of our learning, connecting our experiences and knowledge to make meaning of or solve new puzzles, transforming ourselves and, in the best examples, changing the world in the process.

The Pedagogical Is Political

The pedagogical core is not only the basic structure within which learning happens (or not), but also a basic unit of power relationships, where dominant forms of hierarchical separation and control can be either reproduced or subverted. Rather than perpetuating vertical relationships of power and control (knowledge over teachers, teachers over students), pedagogies that liberate learning establish more horizontal relationships where both parts (teachers and students, students and knowledge) influence each other through dialogue. Individual and collective freedom is not to be pursued solely through the critical examination of and action over our most evident oppressive conditions, but also in the more subtle, everyday interactions between adults and young people in the presence of knowledge.

Good Policy Is Similar to Good Pedagogy

Just as good pedagogy is about establishing relationships of dialogue and mutual learning between students and teachers in the presence of knowledge, good policy is about creating the conditions for educators and system leaders to learn alongside each other about what works and what doesn't in the quest for liberating learning for all students. The worthiness of policy should not be measured by how good it looks on paper or by the extent to which it is implemented with fidelity, but by the extent to which it is developed through a continuous learning partnership between system leaders and schools, whereby both parts learn from and influence each other as they endeavour to fundamentally shift pedagogy and liberate learning.

Schools and Context Should Be Changed in Equal Measure

Changing schools and changing the context that affects students' learning opportunities outside of schools have been treated as two dichotomous options in a zero-sum game – investing in one results in divestment in the other. But there is no reason why the problem has to be framed in this way, especially if pedagogies that liberate learning can take root in schools. Involving communities and cities in educating children and youth, as well as creating opportunities for students to examine local challenges that affect their everyday lives, identifying their key causes and designing and trying out solutions, are some of the ways in which this could be accomplished.

The pedagogies inspired by both Dewey and Freire, when fully embraced and acted upon, are powerful vehicles for liberating learning. There might be important differences in what each of these influential thinkers considers as the key problems to solve. But there is a larger and more important fight to fight than Freire vs. Dewey. It is liberating learning vs. schooling as we have known it. It is about making of the convergence of pedagogies to pursue learning and democracy a new hegemony in the educational change field.

Liberating Learning at Scale

Transforming pedagogy in large numbers of schools and across entire educational systems is one of the greatest challenges of contemporary educational systems around the world. In his classic article "Getting to Scale with Good Educational Practice", Richard Elmore (1996) pointed out that, even in cases where new ideas sought to radically transform teaching and learning in schools and school systems, the pedagogical core had changed very little, noticeable changes occurred in a relatively small number of schools and classrooms, and they didn't last very long in the few places where they were adopted.[14]

More recently, Jal Mehta and Sarah Fine (2015) set out to "map the landscape of non-elite public high schools that are enacting deeper learning" (Mehta & Fine, 2015, p. 10). They used their considerable network to identify and visit schools across the United States. What they found were "startling gaps between aspirations and realities". "We had hoped," they say, "to be inspired but instead we felt profoundly disheartened" (p. 10). They did find individual classrooms here and there where deep learning was alive and well. As a rule of thumb, if they shadowed a student through a regular day in school, about one in every five classes he attended would have some features of a deep learning environment. (And note that these schools were purposefully selected as best examples!)

In summary, most efforts to radically transform pedagogy at scale have so far been difficult, slow, and short lived. But the available evidence can only take us as far as concluding that radical, large-scale pedagogical transformation *has not* occurred. It does not imply that it cannot occur. There is widespread agreement that an effective solution has to be fundamentally different from past educational reform efforts in the United States and internationally (Mehta, Schwartz, & Hess, 2012; Mehta, 2013). As Antonio Gramsci (1971) would put it, we are in a situation of *crisis*, where the old system is dying and the new one is yet to be born.

There are at least three reasons that can explain the failure of previous attempts to change the pedagogical core at scale. The first is a serious underestimation of the resilience of the default culture of schooling and its power to neutralize or devour any serious effort to transform it. The second is the rather weak causal link that most education reforms around the world establish between education policy and the transformation of the pedagogical core. Most reform efforts to transform teaching and learning have sought to change the pedagogical core *from the outside-in* – e.g. changing the curriculum, creating evaluation systems and other external incentives for teachers, investing in new technologies, developing standardized tests to measure student achievement, et cetera – while very seriously underspecifying how exactly these changes will produce substantively improved teaching and learning. A third reason, connected to the second, is a tendency to define and treat the problem of improving teaching and learning as a merely technical problem. As I will further argue throughout this book, the problem of changing pedagogy at scale is not simply a technical matter. It is, more importantly, a cultural and political project. Social movements, rather than large bureaucracies, have historically been the agents of cultural change. In their logic of operation lie the keys to fundamentally changing pedagogy at scale.

As pointed out earlier, transforming the pedagogical core is important not only because it is the most direct way to improve and deepen student learning, but because changing its internal power dynamics is crucial to nurture robust democracies. Like the nucleus of an atom, where tremendous energy resides, huge transformational power lies within the pedagogical core, waiting to be unleashed. When the pedagogical core is changed directly causing deeper student learning, powerful energy is released that can mobilize young people and adults to go deeper and, perhaps more importantly, to spread their liberating learning practice beyond their sites, and to mobilize to change what gets in the way. There are few things as inspiring for educators than seeing their students in a state of *flow* [15] trying to figure out solutions or make meaning of questions that capture their hearts and minds, seeing them continue to work on their own after school and on weekends, witnessing palpable growth in their ability and confidence to learn, or seeing the sparkle in their eye when they figure things out. Liberating learning stimulates the intrinsic motivation of young people and adults alike, it moves them to pursue more and more challenging work and, perhaps more importantly, it propels them to share what they've learned with others. This process is at the core of *liberating learning*, which this book seeks to describe and advance.

Now, this is not as simple as it may sound. Indeed, the idea that you just liberate learning in a few places and it will then organically spread indefinitely to more and more sites is plain naivety. Liberating learning in organizational cultures that are not designed for it and even operate against it is very hard work, with many odds against it. The power of organizational culture to suppress any attempts to change it is, at every step, more likely to prevail than not. As the popular saying goes, culture eats strategy for breakfast.[16] If the century-old history of compulsory schooling is to carry any weight on the future of schooling, the institutional culture and power relationships of schooling have the highest chances to prevail over any attempt to change it.

At the same time, new and fast-paced trends are converging to create powerful conditions for the emergence of radically redefined schools and school systems. First, the possibilities for learning – mostly outside of schools for now – have never been so abundant and easy to access. The invention of the Internet and the fast development of digital technologies put most recorded information available in the world literally at our fingertips (that is, at the fingertips of the privileged half of the world population that has access to the Internet). They have the potential to connect us in real time with millions of people around the world, and open unprecedented opportunities to post our ideas to wide audiences. Thanks to MOOCs (Massive Online Open Access Courses), for example, anyone with an Internet connection and strong enough broadband can access thousands of lectures and courses on a huge variety of topics by professors in some of the best universities in the world. Almost any skill (from sports to playing music to building a space rocket) can now be learned through tutorial videos, available for free on YouTube. Social media allows the rapid spread of ideas and information, and in the right conditions, can make our messages available to millions of people.

These impressive technological developments make these some of the most exciting times for learning. We live in times of abundance of information. Yet, as Will Richardson (2012) reminds us, schools continue to operate as if information were scarce. Something's got to give as the tension grows between a bright future for learning that new technologies are making possible and the rather dull state of learning in most schools around the world.

Second, thanks to machine learning and its rapid evolution, we are a decade or two away from the time when robots will perform and take over activities once considered exclusive of humans – all the way from driving a car to making good medical diagnoses – with greater precision and accuracy than the best human practitioners. It's been a while since the best Jeopardy player in history was badly defeated by IBM's Watson. It's been over a decade since Kasparov, the best living chess player in the world, was defeated at chess by a machine. Take memorization, rational thinking, and any other skill that robots can now do or will be able to do in a few years. Subtract that from what children conventionally learn at school, and you end up with a tiny fraction of – or even negative! – real value. The rise of automation is pushing us to reconsider what it is that humans can excel at that cannot be replaced by machines and that adds value to the world.[17]

While the development of powerful communication technologies is rapidly changing the world of learning outside of schools, there are examples of projects and organizations that have succeeded, at least partially, in either fundamentally transforming teaching and learning, changing pedagogy at scale, or creating system-wide conditions for powerful learning to flourish. There are robust enough bodies of knowledge available that offer us insights and direction for a new educational change paradigm. These include our best available knowledge on educational change; what we currently know about highly successful organizations built around stimulating the internal drive of its members – against the grain of the traditional carrots-and-sticks approach; and what we know about social movements that have acted as powerful vehicles of widespread cultural change.

If scientific management has been the dominant paradigm of educational change in the past, in the new paradigm educational change will be understood and pursued as a social movement; that is, as collective action to pursue a new social order to liberate learning, all the way from individual classrooms to schools and up to entire educational systems. (I will further develop this idea in Chapter 3.) Drawing from growing evidence on pedagogical innovation at small and large scale across the world, this book will present new research evidence to redefine how we understand and promote the widespread transformation of teaching and learning.

The Core Argument of This Book

The core argument developed throughout this book is that radically transforming pedagogy at scale is an endeavour of widespread cultural transformation – that is, a project of fundamentally changing how teachers and students interact with each other in the presence of knowledge, how educators and leaders interact with and transform their institutional surroundings to consolidate and sustain powerful learning and engagement in classrooms, and how policy and practice interact with and influence each other. Social movements have been the most prominent agents of cultural renewal aimed at building more just and democratic societies, and a sustainable world. With this book, I bring the logic of social movements into the realm of formal schooling to advance the radical transformation of teaching and learning at scale, across entire educational systems.

The book integrates knowledge and theory from the fields of large-scale institutional reform and widespread cultural change to advance the notion of educational change as a social movement. In a nutshell, I posit that widespread cultural change in classrooms and schools occurs when new pedagogical practices developed by a critical community are adopted by movements that disseminate them in three arenas: the pedagogical, the social, and the political. I will dedicate one chapter to each of these three arenas. Each chapter, in turn, presents three principles of action to liberate learning in large numbers of schools and across entire educational systems.

The book touches on both the micro-dynamics and the macro-dynamics of pedagogical transformation. Drawing on in-depth case studies of both small-scale and large-scale pedagogical change initiatives, as well as on promising or successful examples of education systems around the world advancing a learning agenda in the social and political arenas, it fleshes out some of the core features of effective and/or innovative pedagogies and looks at how teachers and students learn, perform, and experience these pedagogies in their everyday lives, as well as the wider social and political strategies and conditions that enable their dissemination at scale.

Pedagogies that liberate learning are fundamentally countercultural; that is, they run counter to the instructional culture and power relationships of schooling. They are countercultural because they substantially shift the dynamics within the pedagogical core: from hierarchical relationships of control and authority to horizontal relationships of dialogue, mutual learning, and solidarity. The boundary between teachers and students becomes blurry, with teachers becoming students and students becoming teachers (Hattie, 2009). Students become absorbed in their projects, often losing sense of the passing of time and continuing to explore their burning questions after the school day is over. In-depth conversations and dialogue become a key technology to encourage deep learning: educators and learners engage in close dialogue to make evident what the learner already knows about a topic, identify areas of struggle, and craft questions or point to additional ideas or materials so that the learner can find her own answers. Students help each other when they struggle, asking the teacher for suggestions or comments when necessary. Individual work and cooperation are seamlessly integrated into every classroom activity. Teachers constantly move from group to group, tailoring their one-on-one and group interventions to the emerging needs in the classroom. Sometimes, community participation and a student school government are integrated into the everyday activities, offering multiple opportunities to practise and master democratic behaviours and values.

In a similar vein, leadership practices that liberate learning are also countercultural. The most effective school leaders are no longer those who get everyone to follow their instructions, but those who create the conditions for others to learn while learning alongside them about what works and what doesn't (Fullan, 2014; Robinson, 2011). At the educational system level, it is becoming increasingly evident that what explains success in school districts is effectively managing the relationship between the central office in schools, which entails shifting away from a compliance, command-and-control orientation towards the development of partnerships oriented towards mutual learning and support (Johnson et al., 2015). Effective leadership is thus no longer a merely managerial activity but, most importantly, a pedagogical activity. And it is also political. For one thing, shifting leadership practices from a command-and-control orientation to a mutual learning and support orientation entails changing power dynamics. More broadly, effective school and system leaders manage and tap into their institutional power to support and liberate those they lead, to leverage and partner with those "above" them in the institutional hierarchy, and to connect and collaborate laterally with their peers and the larger community to pursue shared interests.[18]

Today, liberating learning is a relatively scarce phenomenon in schools and school systems. There are, however, a few examples of pedagogical change initiatives that have succeeded in spreading pedagogical change to thousands of schools in the Global South, as well as promising efforts to liberate learning across networks of schools and even across entire school districts in North America. These past and emerging efforts offer important insights into how to advance widespread pedagogical change across entire educational systems. And, more importantly, they call for a new logic to think about and enact educational change.

Structure of the Book

This book is organized into seven chapters. This first chapter has presented an introduction to the book, its purpose, and its core argument. Chapter 2 offers a glimpse into the future of learning, as can be found in some emerging examples of liberating learning in classrooms, schools, and systems. Chapter 3 lays down the theoretical foundations underpinning the core ideas of liberating learning and educational change as social movement. The next three chapters articulate how to advance widespread pedagogical change in three arenas: the pedagogical arena (Chapter 4), the social arena (Chapter 5), and the political arena (Chapter 6). Finally, the closing chapter (Chapter 7) pulls together the core ideas in the book and articulates a call to action.

Notes

1 Only more recently has the phenomenon of learning been looked at directly by educational change scholars. See for example Bellanca (2015); Fullan, Hill, and Rincón-Gallardo (2017), and Mehta and Fine (2015).

2 To be sure, the role of schools as safe environments for children should not be taken for granted. The current epidemic of school shootings and the school-to-prison pipeline affecting thousands of young people of colour in American schools remind us that there is much work yet to be done to ensure that schools, especially in the United States, are safe havens for children and youth.

3 The most recent research article reporting this alarming finding has been published by Makary and Daniel (2016), from the Johns Hopkins University School of Medicine. A good article summarizing and discussing the findings in the paper can be found at: http

s://www.washingtonpost.com/news/to-your-health/wp/2016/05/03/researchers-m
edical-errors-now-third-leading-cause-of-death-in-united-states/?noredirect=on&
utm_term=.99a53b20b69

4 The reported percentages of student enthusiasm decline steadily as grade levels go up. Jenkins (2012) reports that the percentages go up a bit after grade 9 (up to 45 per cent in grade 12). However, he makes three important observations that should warn us against an optimistic interpretation that student enthusiasm increases after grade 9. First, the reported percentages do not include students who dropped out of school after grade 9. Second, students in high school might have a more positive attitude towards school simply because they can see the light at the end of the tunnel. And, third, high school students have more access to elective courses.

5 A couple good books on *neuroplasticity* – the ability of the brain to form or reorganize neuronal networks in response to learning, experience, or following injury – are Michael Merzenich's *Soft-Wired: How the New Science of Brain Plasticity Can Change Your Life* (Merzenich, 2013) and Norman Doidge's *The Brain that Changes Itself* (Doidge, 2007). A good take on how the brain of children works and matures can be found on Daniel Siegel and Tina Payne Bryson's *The Whole-Brain Child* (Siegel & Payne Bryson, 2012).

6 The ideas in this paragraph are drawn from a reflection paper by Richard Elmore (2016), where he connects findings from the neuroscience of learning and architectural designs for learning with his take on the *tutorial networks* model developed and spread across thousands of schools in Mexico.

7 "Instructional core" is the actual concept coined by David Cohen and colleagues (Cohen et al., 2003) and later on taken up by City, Elmore, Fiarman, and Teitel (2009). I prefer to use "pedagogy" instead of "instruction" to refer to the relationship between educator and learner in the presence of knowledge. The term instruction implies a clear vertical relationship of authority and control between educator and learner, whereas pedagogy allows for other forms of relationships. More on this in Chapter 3.

8 See for example *Instructional Rounds* by City, Elmore, Fiarman, and Teitel (2009) and *Intentional Interruption* by Katz and Dack (2012).

9 In his book *Absolutism and the Eighteenth-Century Origins of Compulsory Schooling*, James van Horn Melton (2003) examines the origins, purpose, and achievements of two compulsory school movements during the reigns of Frederick the Great of Prussia (1740–1786) and Maria Theresa of Austria (1740–1780). The author demonstrates that compulsory schooling was part of a broader campaign to strengthen relationships of authority and dependence between rulers and society.

10 The ideas in this section were first published in the Education Week's *Learning Deeply Blog* edited by Jal Mehta and Robert Rothman (Rincón-Gallardo, 2017). Due to editorial decisions unknown to me, the post ended up being titled "Three Theories of Educational Change". The original title, which in my view captures more accurately the central argument and the ideas presented in the post, was: "Dewey and Freire Need Each Other to Fight a Common Enemy: Conventional Schooling." The blog post can be found at: http://blogs.edweek.org/edweek/learning_deeply/2017/07/dewey_and_freire_need_ea ch_other_to_fight_a_greater_enemy_conventional_schooling.html

11 For examples of unexpected schools in the United States, see Chenoweth (2007, 2009), and Meier (2002). Examples from the Global South can be found in Colbert and Arboleda (2016), Niesz and Krishnamurthy (2013, 2014), Rincón-Gallardo, (2016, 2017), and Zaalouk (2006).

12 See *Excellence through Equity* (Blankstein, Noguera, & Kelly, 2016; OECD, 2013).

13 It should be noted that the Freire and Dewey siloes, as presented here, are represented by two men. Male dominance in the educational change and social justice fields is perhaps one of the reasons why these siloes exist in the first place. There are equally powerful women educators who have advanced progressive education and critical pedagogies. The

Freire–Dewey divide, for example, could also be named the bell hooks–Maria Montessori divide. I will keep the Freire–Dewey terminology for purposes of simplicity. But this section could equally be called *bell hooks meets Maria Montessori.*

14 To develop his argument, Elmore examines the progressive education movement in the United States, a fertile era of innovation that saw the creation of individual schools that exemplified progressive pedagogies and several attempts to promote progressive pedagogical practices at scale in public school systems. Making reference to Larry Cuban's (1984) study of the impact of large-scale reforms of curriculum and pedagogy in schools and classrooms in the United States between 1890 and 1980, Elmore points out that the new student-centred pedagogies advanced by the progressive movement "seldom appeared in more than one-fourth of the classrooms in any district that systematically tried to install [progressive education]" (Cuban, 1984, p. 135, in Elmore, 1996). Furthermore, "even in settings where teachers made a conscious effort to incorporate progressive practices, the result was often hybrid of traditional and progressive, where the major elements of the traditional core of instruction remained largely undisturbed" (Elmore, 1996, p. 9).

15 The phenomenon of *flow* was first identified and studied systematically by Mihaly Csikszentmihalyi (1990). Flow is an optimal state of intrinsic motivation, where people are so immersed in an activity that nothing else seems to matter.

16 While the original source of this quote is uncertain, it is attributed to late business management guru, Peter Drucker. Mark Fields, former president of Ford, is credited for popularizing the phrase (it is said that it was among his favourite slogans).

17 For a good, deeper discussion of these trends, see Daniel Pink's (2006) *A Whole New Mind: Why Right Brainers Will Rule the Future*, Martin Ford's (2016) *Rise of the Robots*, Klaus Schwab's (2016) *The Fourth Industrial Revolution*, and Derek Thompson's (2015) *A World Without Work.*

18 This is what Andy Hargreaves and Michael Fullan refer to as *Leadership from the Middle* (Hargreaves & Fullan, 2012). The concept was originally coined by Andy Hargreaves and Henry Braun in their case study about a handful of districts in Ontario that took on the responsibility to figure out solutions to the problem of low student outcomes and unequal educational opportunities for students with special needs (Hargreaves & Braun, 2012). Among other things, the authors found that, during a time of lack of cohesive leadership at the top of the Ministry of Education, these school districts offered leadership for the system, interacting *laterally* among each other, providing support *downward* to schools, and leveraging *upward* with the Ministry of Education. The concept of Leadership from the Middle has been further developed and explained in Fullan (2015a) and Hargreaves and Aiscow (2015).

2

A GLIMPSE INTO THE FUTURE OF LEARNING

In many ways, the future of learning is already here. The Internet and the explosion of digital technologies allow immediate access to information, at least for the half of the world population with access to the Internet. They enable people and organizations to communicate and collaborate across national and regional borders. They facilitate the connection between experts in a variety of fields and avid learners. Massive Online Open Access Courses, or MOOCs, make it possible for anyone with an Internet connection to take and complete courses on almost any imaginable topic, for free, from professors in Ivy League universities; YouTube has now a massive archive of tutorial videos to learn almost any skill you can think of, all the way from playing the ukulele to building a 3-D printer from scratch. Online communication allows the creation of robust networks of widely diverse individuals and organizations who are solving problems once considered impossible, from quickly and reliably locating missing objects across an entire country, to stopping the spread of epidemics or demonstrating mathematical theorems once thought unsolvable (see Nielsen, 2012 or Pentland, 2014).

In stark contrast with the fast-paced spread and growth of digital technologies for learning, the basic grammar of schooling has remained practically stable for over a century. Some leading education thinkers are now suggesting that the future of learning will flourish outside of schools, while schools might continue to exist mostly to provide custody and care for children and youth. Others have suggested that if schools fail to nurture deep learning and durable learning skills among our younger generations, they will be substituted with different, more effective and agile institutions. Whether or not most schools and school systems around the world will succeed at becoming vibrant places for learning remains an open question.

While facing many odds, I am convinced that the pursuit of renewed public education systems that embrace and build movements to liberate learning is worth our best efforts. In this chapter, I will offer a glimpse into liberating learning, as can be observed in a handful of classrooms, schools, and school systems around the world.

Liberating Learning in Classrooms

There are reasons for optimism. Throughout the history of compulsory schooling, and to this date, examples can be found of classrooms, schools, and school systems organized around liberating learning for young people and adults alike. Some contemporary examples offer us glimpses into the future of learning. Some of these examples come from the Global South, a region often overlooked by scholars of educational change. Others come from developed economies.

LIBERATING LEARNING IN CLASSROOMS (THREE EXAMPLES)

In a digital media class in central California high school, students plan and run a live recording of a soccer match. Some capture the match through multiple video cameras, others coordinate the projection of the live show in real time, others narrate the game live, others design and run live interviews with the players at the end of the game, and so on. The same group has been broadcasting a weekly TV show, produced and managed by students themselves. The focus, skill, and coordination of these young people, as well as the high quality of the work they produce, often make external observers forget for a moment they're in a school and believe instead that they are witnessing a full-fledged professional recording team in action.

***

In a fully equipped cafeteria kitchen, a group of high school students in Sault-Saint Marie, in the province of Ontario, prepare meals to feed between 300 and 400 students and a few adults each day. Led by the chef (also a high school student), and only with a light-touch supervision of a professional chef, they run the full operation of the cafeteria: all the way from designing the menu, to finding locally sourced ingredients, to preparing and cooking the dishes, to maintaining the kitchen clean and functional. They do this every weekday for two hours a day – and this work counts for credit towards their high school diploma. This group of students caters to many community and school events. The food they serve is so good that principals from other schools come here for breakfast or lunch, and the cafeteria team is often hired to cater to school and community events. They now have plans to start and run a bistro that will open to the larger public. When asked what they're learning from running the kitchen, students respond with remarkable eloquence about skills that range from so-called soft-skills such as maintaining calm and focus under high stress, keeping focus for prolonged periods of time, working in teams (for example, learning to rely and develop faith that everyone here is doing their part), self-confidence (knowing you're able to do well in things you didn't think you were good at), communicating clearly and being aware of what each person in the group is up to, problem-solving in real time as it arises in the kitchen, time management, to more specific knowledge and skills, such as how to prepare a meal, how to use a knife properly, and the nuances of restaurant cooking that make it different from home-cooking, the ability to manage a much larger scale of meal preparation without losing quality.

***

In a one-classroom multi-grade middle school in rural Mexico, students are working individually or in small groups on inquiry projects of their choice – selected from a collection of topics that at least one tutor in the group has mastered in their own network of tutors. The students work at their own pace, moving freely inside the classroom and around the school to search for books or other materials, to discuss ideas with a colleague or the teacher. The place buzzes in activity, and everyone seems highly focused on their work. The two teachers in the school walk around and stop for moments to engage in dialogue with individual students about the work they're doing and how they're learning. More than explaining things, tutors ask questions to discern how students are thinking about the problem or topic at hand, and use this knowledge to support the students to make sense of what they don't yet understand. The students demonstrate what and how they're learning in writing and in public presentations to the group and the larger community. Later on, they are expected to serve as tutors to other students interested in learning about the topic they now master. In these learning communities, the roles of student and tutor are in constant flux. Sometimes teachers are tutors to students, others students tutor each other, and yet other times students are tutors of teachers.

Walk into a place where liberating learning is regular practice and you will find students working individually or in small groups on problems or questions that matter to them, over extended periods of time. You will see each student working at their own pace and in the space of their choice – in one of many work stations set up in a classroom, in hallways, or outdoors. No assigned sitting, no rows of individual chairs and desks, very little – if any – time spent on adult lectures for the whole group. Some kids may work on tables; others sit or lie on their bellies on a carpet to read; others on rocking chairs, cushiony seats, couches, a foyer in the hallway; yet others stand up next to each other while discussing a text, a personal note, or figuring out how an artefact of interest works.

You will hear a constant buzz made up of the multiple conversations taking place, most of them centred around the work students are doing, the questions or dilemmas they're facing, or the strategies they're using to make sense of their topics of study. While there is a constant flow of people and conversation, everyone seems highly focused on their work. In fact, if you come to a place like this as an external observer, the people in the group will likely not notice you're there until you come closer to see their work and hear what they're saying. You will also notice that students seem unaware of time passing – they may be surprised when the time for recess or the end of the day comes. They continue their work during recess, at home, or on weekends. Students there work harder, but they don't seem to mind. They actually seem to *want* to work harder.

Approach any of the students in these classrooms and ask them about their work, and they will be able to articulate, on the spot and with remarkable clarity, what they are doing and why, what they are learning and how, why it matters, to what extent they've gained mastery of what they're learning, what are key areas where they need to get better at, and their plans to do just that. They may show you with pride some of the work they've produced, pointing to parts of it as they explain their learning. Ask them what they think about this way of working and you will hear genuine signs of excitement and self-efficacy.

Look for some examples of student work and learning tools being used in the classroom and you will start to see the varied ways in which students connect with the outside world as part of their regular activities. If the school you visit is equipped with Internet and devices to access it, you may see blogs, podcasts, or videos produced by the students to make their learning visible to wider audiences. Many students may use an Internet browser to search for information or digital tools they need to make sense of the questions they're tackling. You may find evidence of exchange with experts in the fields that students are learning about – either because the experts visit the school, meeting with the class virtually to provide feedback, or because students visit them in their workplace to gain exposure to their expert practice.

Now pay attention to the colour of the skin, the gender identity, or the physical mobility of students in the group. You may be surprised – for it is unusual – that the quality and degree of challenge of the work being done and the treatment from other peers and adults remains equally demanding and respectful no matter what the student looks like.

Follow one or more adults in the room and observe their interactions with students. Teachers move across the multiple learning spaces to engage in one-on-one or small group conversation with students. They constantly ask students to articulate what they are doing and why, offering specific feedback to their work. They listen attentively to what students have to say and remain alert to evidence of what they have learned, how they are thinking about the problem at hand, to what extent they are transferring knowledge and skills learned previously to tackle a new situation, or what misconceptions, mistakes, or dilemmas remain unresolved. Only after careful listening do they offer feedback, ask a carefully crafted question to help students find their own answers, or suggest possible next steps. Adults make themselves available to respond when a student has a question or feels stuck, and intervene when conflict or another problem arises in a group of students working together. Whole group activities are brief and agile, used to make announcements for the class or to share insights or questions from individual students and small groups with the larger group. In a group like this, you will see spontaneous signs of affection between teachers and students – a tap on the shoulder, a smile, a joke, a big laugh.

In places like this, adults are constantly learning in public: perhaps by saying "I don't know" when they don't have an answer to a question asked by a student; by learning about a topic or how to use a digital learning tool from a student who masters it; by making mistakes in public, acknowledging and correcting them; by expressing genuine surprise and excitement when a student comes up with a good solution or idea that they had not thought about; by acknowledging confusion and going through it in public; by expressing aloud how and what they're thinking when going through a puzzling question or problem; or by publicly opening their most hard-wired assumptions to scrutiny.

Liberating Learning in Schools

If you happen to be in one of those unlikely sites where liberating learning is embraced by, and nurtured in, the whole school on a regular basis, shadow a teacher for a day. You will become aware of the multiple occasions on which she interacts – formally and informally – with her colleagues and the principal to talk about and strategize around pedagogy and student learning. It won't take long to notice that, just as students, teachers have multiple opportunities to experience liberating learning in their everyday work. Teacher and principal learning is a constant and highly visible activity in these schools. Adults in the school may be offered the time and space to explore topics or learn to use tools that they're not too familiar with. They will have allocated time to meet regularly with their colleagues to work in teams, either by grade or in cross-panel fashion – teachers from multiple grades in elementary schools, or from multiple departments in intermediate or secondary school. In these teams, they co-plan and co-design common learning activities, analyse student work, assess whether and how deeply students are learning, examine pedagogical practices in light of these assessments, and continuously devise, test, and refine their strategies to enhance and deepen student learning. As with students, if you ask them about their work, teachers will be able to explain with eloquence what their students are doing and why, to what extent and how deeply they're learning, how they know this, what is working and what isn't in their current practice, and what are their plans to get better. And it won't take much effort to perceive a genuine sense of excitement, pride, and hope in their words and expressions.

Visit the school for a few days in a row and you will notice the active role parents play in the learning of their children. Parent meetings are mostly focused on student learning – for example, to discuss what students are expected to know and be able to do as a result of going to the school, to look at evidence of student learning, or to clarify why the work students are doing is so different from the schooling experience of parents. Administrative and logistical announcements use up only a minimal part of the agenda.

You will realize that the notes sent home by the teachers are way more often to request parents to discuss with their kids a topic they're exploring than they are to remind them to complete menial tasks.

LIBERATING LEARNING IN A SCHOOL[1]

In a public high school in Ontario, Canada, a group of students is working on building a bridge, using cardboard as their only material, that can carry a person of average weight. Students here have no pre-determined schedule. Each of them determines how to use their time throughout the day, what do to, and with whom. Yet they are remarkably organized and focused. When asked about their work, the depth of their knowledge of physics, mathematics, and engineering stands out, as does their confidence to speak to strangers, their skill to learn independently and in teams, and their joy of learning.

This is the Research and Development group (R&D), with a focus on science and engineering. In this school, the principal and his staff have been experimenting with credit bundling as a means of creating deep learning environments within the school. Another credit bundle is EnviroVentures, which combines courses on practical life skills, language, and social sciences. It's a whole day credit programme where students spend full days together throughout the semester, each managing their time and focus throughout the day according to their learning needs and preferences. They also travel together on outdoor excursions that are a part of the programme's outdoor education component. Just like in R&D, the emphasis is on learning by doing. EnviroVentures students spend full days together engaged in learning tasks, sometimes individually, other times in small groups. Successful completion of the work in these groups leads to four grade 11 university-level credits.

In these two credit-bundle groups, the atmosphere is electric, alive with the spirit of learning. Students are passionate about and visibly invested in their learning and they understand their role in the learning of their peers. When students speak of their school and their peers, they use words such as "family", "friendship", and "support". They talk about facing and tackling challenges together, whether it be hiking the last kilometres of a day-long hike in the pouring rain or solving the building of a cardboard bridge that must hold 150-pounds load. "In a conventional class," one student said, "[there are] no smiles. In Enviro, it's a completely different feeling. People love where they are."

In the R&D group, students demonstrate remarkable depth of understanding of physics, mathematics, engineering. They display confidence and comfort, regulating their own learning and navigating and overcoming uncertainty and complexity. When explaining examples of problems they had been tackling over the semester (e.g. constructing a slide system on the classroom walls that maximized the time it would take a metal ball to roll down it, or building a cardboard bridge strong enough to carry a person), each student is able to articulate, on the spot and with remarkable clarity, sophistication, and confidence, what the problem was, what their most important attempts were and what made them weak or strong, and the core principles of physics, engineering, and mathematics at play. Furthermore, they talk about how they had been using time outside of school to think about these problems more deeply. One young woman in the group, for example, says that she and her peers can no longer go past a bridge without stopping – sometimes literally getting out of the bus – to think about its design, why it was designed the way it was, and what would have been other possible ways to build it. One young man said he got so obsessed with bridge building that he worked for weeks in figuring out how to build, in his own time, a bridge built with popsicle sticks only, that could carry him.

Liberating Learning in Districts

Now, if you're lucky enough to be in one of those very rare places where an entire school district is organized around powerful learning for students and adults alike, you will see that a vision for deep student learning is embedded in every aspect of the district's work. This vision is used as the basic point of reference to orient the work of the system, to review existing initiatives, to let go of those not aligned with the core vision, and to develop and select strategies to liberate learning across the system. District leaders and staff will be able to articulate with specificity and precision what powerful learning looks like in action, what are key observable features of the pedagogical practices that liberate learning, and how their most prominent activities as district leaders connect to improved teacher practice and deeper student learning. You will identify a wide range of supports and conditions that the districts offer to the adults in the system to experience liberating learning themselves and to change their practice to liberate learning with their students.

You may find material expressions of the system's commitment to powerful learning in the architecture and organization of learning spaces across the district (see vignette, "Liberating Learning across an Entire District").

You will see district leaders and staff acting as "lead learners", that is, as leaders who create the conditions for everyone to learn while learning alongside them about what works and what doesn't. You will see them engaged in joint work – with their colleagues, with school leaders and educators alike – to examine, try out, test, and continuously refine pedagogical practice in classrooms. You will hear constant messages encouraging teachers and students to try and do things differently, to fail, learn from failure, and get better over time. People across the system will tell you that their school and district are places where they feel safe to experiment, make mistakes, and constantly get better as a result.

And you will see district leaders learning in public. You might see them learning from kids in student-led workshops or tutoring sessions to learn how to leverage digital devices and resources to enhance learning. They participate in learning walks to constantly refine their skill to observe classroom practice and offer teachers useful feedback focused on improving and deepening the learning of students and adults alike. And they meet periodically with school leaders to share and develop solutions to their problems of practice.

You will notice that in systems like these, leadership and power are distributed and remarkably flat: Teachers and school leaders have direct access to a senior leader in the central office, and system leaders intentionally interact with actors in the system through dialogue, open communication, and joint development of solutions. Across the board, you will see signs of system coherence, or the shared depth of understanding about the nature of the work (Fullan & Quinn, 2015). In your conversations with people across the system, all the way from classrooms to the central office, you will notice consistent narratives in their talk about the core priorities of the district, the key strategies to pursue those priorities, and the specific ways in which their everyday work connects to the priorities and strategies of the system.

LIBERATING LEARNING ACROSS AN ENTIRE DISTRICT[2]

The Ottawa Catholic School Board (OCSB) in Ontario is a system where learning – of students and adults alike – is visible at every layer of the district's activities. Let's take a look, layer by layer, from the inside out. In some of the schools leading the way on pedagogical innovation and learning environments in this district, you can see elementary school kids moving freely within and between three or four rooms over extended blocks of time, working individually or in small groups on tasks of their choice – either selected from a variety of tasks carefully designed by a team of teachers or co-created by students and teachers – constantly presenting and refining their ideas to their peers and the adults in the room. Tasks and questions students embark on vary widely, and include things like:

a. *exploring how to re-establish beauty in the world, fleshing out essential and divergent views of beauty, designing and implementing plans to re-establish beauty in their school and community;*

b. *grade 10 students interviewing and interacting with grade 1 students, asking for pictures, videos of themselves and their families, what they like, to create narratives capturing who these young people are;*

c. *grade 2 students engaging in all stages of creating a school garden, from reaching agreement and planning around what to grow, what to do with the produce, pros and cons of each alternative, creating the garden, and maintaining it throughout the year;*

d. *students creating video games with the support and feedback of an expert video game designer.*

e. *Students creating a totem that represents them individually, with presentation and assistance from a First Nations elder.*

In these schools, there is a learning function in almost every aspect of the school building. Learning commons offer room for study and collaboration, with ample space to walk around, movable furniture, projectors that students can access at any time, and tablets and other digital devices for borrowing. There is Wi-Fi across the entire building. Students are allowed to and often bring in and work with their personal devices. Floors in the hallways have different sections painted in different colours indicating which areas are for work and which are for circulation. There are green walls through the building for students to record videos to which they can later add moving or still backgrounds. There are small glass-covered holes in the walls here and there that reveal the internal structure of the building, with barcodes that can be scanned to find information about that part of the building structure and how it functions. Colourful student-made art is displayed across the hallways, in the form of large murals on the walls, painted panels encrusted on the ceilings, or posted on large boards.

Teacher and principal learning is a constant and highly visible activity in these schools and across the district. Teachers meet often to work in teams, either by grade or in cross-panel fashion to co-plan and co-design common learning activities, examine student work to identify depth of understanding of the topics at hand and the degree of development of core skills such as colla- boration and citizenship, identify areas of improvement, and constantly refine their practice. But the visibility of teacher learning is not confined to teacher collaboration during prep and planning time. It carries over to classrooms. There are schools where learning alongside or directly from students has become part of the regular activities of teachers, either to explore ideas or questions students come up with that teachers themselves don't know the answers to, or to learn to use new digital devices or resources teachers are not familiar with.

Principals and district administrators also learn in public. They attend student- led workshops or tutoring sessions to learn how to leverage digital devices and resources to enhance their own learning and improve their pedagogical and leadership practice; they participate in learning walks to constantly refine their skill to observe classroom practice, and offer teachers useful feedback focused on improving their practice and deepening student learning. Every month, all princi- pals attend a Catholic Learning Leaders meeting, together with district coordina- tors and superintendents, to share and develop solutions to their problems of practice; and, as reported by teachers, principals also model learning in their meetings with staff – as an elementary school principal said: "In staff meetings the principal is only one of the voices on the table. It is very common that teacher voice subsides that of the principal."

OCSB has managed to literally put deep learning front and centre of its efforts. A graphic that places six deep learning competencies (Collaboration, Commu- nication, Creativity, Critical Thinking, Character, and Citizenship) at the centre, surrounded by the four elements of Pedagogical Practices, Learning Partnerships, Learning Environments, and Leveraging Digital has been designed and distributed across the entire school district, and can be found everywhere from the board room in the central office to school and classroom walls. But, far beyond the graphic, the most remarkable accomplishment of OCSB lies in its purposeful creation of an organizational culture where deep learning lives in the minds and hearts of growing numbers of people in all 83 schools in the system, and all the way from classroom to the central office.

The district leadership at OCSB operates as a remarkably flat structure, which allows robust two-way communication between the central office and schools. A coherence committee has been created to maintain a constant flow of communication and collaboration between all the units that make up the district, avoid the duplication of efforts, and to work on defining with increasing clarity how the key actions of the central office are supporting the development and spread of pedagogies that liberate learning across the system.

Liberating Learning across Thousands of Schools

Now, imagine visiting a nation or a state where liberating learning has spread to thousands of schools, across entire educational systems. What you will find are examples of lively and strong movements of pedagogical change where everyone, all the way from students and teachers to state and national leaders, maintains a relentless focus on fostering learner-centred pedagogies, with a special emphasis on reaching the most remote and historically marginalized communities across the territory. Talk to actors across the system and they will be able to articulate, with remarkable clarity and simplicity, what are the core features of their pedagogical practice, why they decided to adopt it, and the profound effect it has had in their own lives and the lives of their students. You will witness the strong presence that parents and the larger community have in the everyday lives of the schools involved. This might be evident in the presence of parents during public demonstrations where students showcase what and how they're learning; in the participation of parents as mentors in their areas of expertise; or in the creation of community development projects designed and run with the active participation of students. Across the entire system, you will hear expressions of pride and hope coming from the shared feeling that those involved, all the way from children to teachers to system leaders, are learning better and feel part of a cause larger than themselves. Furthermore, ask about trends in student outcomes and you will likely find that schools involved in movements of this kind are improving student outcomes at a faster pace than schools serving more privileged students. This will be the case despite the fact that improving test scores is barely present in the purposes and the everyday work of movement participants.

CASE 2.1 LEARNING COMMUNITY PROJECT[3]

The Learning Community Project (LCP) has its origins in the work and ideas of Gabriel Cámara, former Jesuit priest who in the 1970s developed close friendship with Paulo Freire and Ivan Illich, two of the most well-known critics of schooling and proponents of emancipatory education in Latin America.

In LCP schools, each student chooses a topic of inquiry from a catalogue of topics that at least one tutor in the group masters. The student follows an individual line of inquiry with the support of the tutor, who supports the learning process by identifying and leveraging what the student already knows, pointing out relevant information within the text being reviewed or in other sources, or crafting and asking good questions to allow the student to find their own answers. Students demonstrate publicly what and how they're learning – in writing and in public presentations to the group, and often to parents and the larger community. Once a student masters a topic, they are expected to become tutors to students interested in learning it. In a learning community, the roles of tutor and learner are in constant flux. Who is a tutor and who is a learner is not determined by the formal role assigned in the school, but by who masters a topic and who is interested in learning it. Sometimes adults serve as tutors of students, other times students tutor each other, and yet other times students are tutors of adults.

LCP started in 2003 as a grass-roots, small-scale pedagogical change project in a handful of multi-grade rural middle schools in two states in Mexico. It was originally designed and led by a small non-government organization called *Convivencia Educativa, A.C.* (now *Redes de Tutoría/ Aprender con Interés*), with funding from the Inter-American Development Bank as part of the Partnership for the Revitalization of Education in the Americas (PREAL). Over the next six years, LCP grew from a handful to a few dozen schools through the outreach, organizing and networking participating teachers, local communities, local educational authorities, and project leaders. In 2009, LCP was adopted by the Ministry of Education and expanded first to a couple hundred schools in 10 states through a two-year pilot project, and then nationally to 9,000 public schools with a history of underperformance. In this phase of nation-wide expansion, LCP's core pedagogy was adopted as the centre-piece of a larger strategy for school improvement, first called the Program for Improvement of Educational Achievement (PEMLE for its initials in Spanish) and later on the Integral Strategy for the Improvement of Educational Achievement (EIMLE).

During the years of LCP's early expansion, Dalila López, a key leader of LCP during its grass-roots stage, was invited to join the Department of Innovation at the Ministry of Education. When the Ministry adopted LCP, Dalila was asked to lead the efforts to spread its pedagogy to a few hundred and later on to thousands of schools. In her new position, Dalila started to recruit leaders of LCP into her team, creating a hybrid leadership team that combined people with practical expertise on pedagogical change and people with deep knowledge of the bureaucracy within the Ministry of Education. Under Dalila's leadership, the nationwide effort to spread tutorial networks to thousands of schools maintained a strong link between design and execution. National leaders of the programme took on the responsibility to demonstrate that it was possible to bring to the everyday life of classrooms and schools the pedagogy they advocated for. This created a culture where everyone involved, regardless of their institutional position, was expected to master and model LCP's core pedagogical practice as part of their regular work.

Thanks to EIMLE, public middle schools in the communities with the highest degrees of marginalization completed middle school and enrolled in high school at much higher rates, and improved student achievement at a faster pace than and surpassing public schools serving more privileged youth in regular public schools.

If you talk to system leaders involved in these movements, you will discover that their discourse and leadership practice are remarkably different from that of a bureaucrat in a conventional public education system. They are very familiar with – if not living examples of – the pedagogies for liberating learning that they seek to nurture and spread. They know the bureaucracy well and have learned how to leverage its infrastructure to facilitate the widespread dissemination of the new pedagogies. They are finding ways to change the institutional logic of the system where they operate, leaving behind vertical relationships of authority and control over schools, and nurturing instead horizontal relationships of dialogue, co-learning, and mutual influence between the central leadership and schools. They spend a lot of time in schools and classrooms, not to evaluate teachers and principals, but to assess whether and how the strategy of widespread pedagogical change is working (or not) and to identify what needs to be changed, refined, or discarded for a more effective strategy.

There are examples of movements of this type, although not so much in the places where the educational change field has been looking – in so-called developed economies such as Australia, Canada, England, Finland, Japan, Singapore, or the United States. The most powerful examples of pedagogical change movements reaching thousands of schools come from the Global South – the regions of the world that share a history of colonialism, often called "developing countries" or the "Third World".

CASE 2.2 ESCUELA NUEVA IN COLOMBIA[4]

Escuela Nueva was created in the mid-1970s by an unlikely trio of education pioneers: Vicky Colbert (a social entrepreneur), Oscar Mogollón (an outstanding teacher in a rural, multi-grade school in Colombia), and Beryl Levinger (a USAID education officer). With the intention of universalizing primary education in rural areas, especially in isolated multi-grade schools, Escuela Nueva adopted core pedagogical principles of progressive educators such as John Dewey, Maria Montessori, Jean Piaget, and Lev Vygotsky and turned them into strategies to make active, child-centred, and participatory pedagogies available to small, rural schools across Colombia.

In Escuela Nueva, children of different ages work in the same room, individually and in small groups, using self-learning guides designed to simultaneously grant access to relevant information and core ideas from the national curriculum and to nurture habits of independent learning, peer tutoring, and teamwork. Students move freely within the room to access the information and resources they need when they need them. A flexible promotion mechanism allows students to complete learning units at their own pace, and to move from one grade to another based on their progress and needs, rather than on their age. As part of their everyday work, students observe, reflect, write individually and in small groups, review and correct their drafts, and self-assess their work and their learning process. Teachers move within the room to work with individual students or small groups, offering feedback and suggestions based on the work students are producing. Their role is that of guides and facilitators of learning.

The learning environment is carefully organized in different sections that students can access anytime: a school library; a learning corner with multiple materials, resources, and tools to support meaning-making and the construction of artefacts and devices to showcase what students are learning; and movable furniture that allows for multiple table configurations for individual work and collaboration in small groups.

Every Escuela Nueva has a student government, whose officers are chosen by vote in elections organized and run by the students themselves. The student government makes decisions on the direction and activities of the school, mediates conflict between students, stays attuned and responds to emerging concerns in the school, and serves as a link between school and community. Community and family participation are another key component of the Escuela Nueva model. Students are expected to identify local problems and design and test solutions, while parents and other members of the community are invited to teach students about local traditions and activities.

The origins of Escuela Nueva go back to the mid-1970s. At the time, Vicky Colbert was the national coordinator of the Unitary School in the Ministry of

Education, a programme initiated by UNESCO in Colombia. In her trips across the country she met Oscar Mogollón, a teacher who ran an exemplary unitary school in the province of Norte de Santander, under the UNESCO project. With the support of the Ministry of Education's Department of Planning, and with initial funding from USAID, Vicky Colbert, Oscar Mogollón, and Beryl Levinger set out to design a system-wide strategy to make the best ideas and pedagogical practices of the Unitary School project more viable technically, politically, and financially, with the intention of spreading it to more multi-grade schools around the country. They incorporated new operational strategies that went beyond the concept of multi-grade schools, and introduced a more child-centred, participatory approach, as well as a new role of the teacher as facilitator, mentor, and guide. The strategy also included principles of classroom organization, as well as the active involvement of administrators and local communities.

In the late 1970s, an innovation project was initiated in three regions of Colombia. In 1976, Colbert was appointed the first national coordinator of Escuela Nueva at the Ministry of Education. She built her team with outstanding rural teachers in multi-grade schools she had met in her multiple trips across the country. As part of the strategy, Colbert and her team led the creation of demonstration schools and organized a network of rural teachers for exchange and continuous professional learning. Over the next decade, Escuela Nueva expanded to about 3,000 schools with the financial support of provincial governments, the Inter-American Development Bank, and *Fundación para la Educación Superior* (FES) in Cali.

In the mid-1980s, Colbert was appointed Deputy Minister of Education, and Oscar Mogollón became the national coordinator of Escuela Nueva. The access of key leaders of Escuela Nueva to institutional power enhanced their capacity to protect the team and the technical continuity of the process of consolidating pedagogical innovation on the ground and spreading it to a significantly greater number of schools. In 1985, the government decided to adopt Escuela Nueva as the strategy to universalize primary education in rural areas. The model further expanded to 8,000 schools across the country. Between 1987 and 1992, with funding from the World Bank, Escuela Nueva reached 20,000 rural schools across Colombia.

Thanks to Escuela Nueva, by the year 2000 Colombia was second only to Cuba in terms of the educational quality available to rural schools in Latin America, with students in Escuela Nueva outperforming their counterparts in urban settings (except for the mega cities of Colombia). Furthermore, students in Escuela Nueva showed stronger citizenship values and practices than did students in conventional schools.

In 1989, the World Bank selected Escuela Nueva as one of the three most outstanding reforms in developing countries. In the year 2000, the Human Development Report in Colombia selected Escuela Nueva as one of the country's main achievements. Vicky Colbert has received several recognitions as an outstanding social entrepreneur, including the WISE Prize in Quatar in 2013, and more recently the inaugural Yidan Prize for Education Development, considered by some the "Nobel Prize" of Education, in 2017.

Charles Leadbeater (2012) has pointed out that the most powerful innovations in education are not coming from developed economies, but from the Global South. This is so because in so-called emerging economies needs are greatest, unmet demand is huge, and conventional solutions are too expensive and ineffective. It seems, like the old saying goes, that necessity is indeed the mother of invention. Looked at from this perspective, the Global South is leading the way when it comes to reimagining and reinventing public education systems. To be sure, the three cases featured in this section have had important flaws and shortcomings, stories of scaling-down, sudden marginalization from the educational systems where they've operated, or bureaucratization of their original and organic pedagogies in many sites. However, their genesis and development as social movements aimed at fundamentally transforming teaching and learning across thousands of schools, and their relative success in enhancing student learning at scale, are worth our attention.

CASE 2.3 ACTIVITY BASED LEARNING MODEL IN TAMIL NADU, INDIA[5]

Activity Based Learning (ABL) is an approach to primary education (grades 1–4) that spread to all of the 37,000 primary government schools in the state of Tamil Nadu in South India between 2003 and 2010. Many of the children attending these schools live in poverty and belong to the Dalit caste in India, referred to in the past as "untouchables". ABL is grounded on a philosophy of learning that sees and treats children as full-on autonomous and purposeful learners. Organized in multi-age classrooms, children move freely, gathering materials and working on learning activities on their own, in small groups, or with the teacher. Teachers move across the room, sitting on floor mats to work alongside kids. The work is structured in carefully designed learning activities organized in a learning "ladder" that is posted in the classroom for everyone to see, and which students consult independently, while searching for and reviewing, at their own pace and whenever they need them, the child-friendly texts and materials available in the room, which include slim, colourful picture books hanging on clotheslines across the room, colourful bins of learning cards, and other didactic materials. Every ABL classroom has a chalkboard that runs across its whole perimeter and extends from the floor to the height of the children, for kids to use as they please to sketch ideas or solutions and discuss them with their peers or with the teacher. Frontal lectures, textbooks, and traditional examinations (strong defining elements of the school culture in India) are nowhere to be found in ABL classrooms.

Since the large-scale rollout of ABL in 2007, government schools in Tamil Nadu saw dramatic improvements in school attendance and gender parity. Remarkable differences were reported in the confidence and efficacy of students before and after ABL – from shy, quiet, passive, and submissive children to highly active, confident, and eloquent learners. Reports measuring impact on student outcomes are mixed and inconclusive, and some critics have pointed out that according to nationwide learning achievement surveys students in Tamil Nadu are reaching only average levels of performance. This reservation notwithstanding, Tamil Nadu is a relevant example of widespread dissemination of a set of pedagogical practices that run counter to the conventional culture of schools – in India and internationally.

ABL was weaved through long-lasting and growing partnerships between agents of the state – most prominently M.P. Vijayakumar – activists from people's movements, and progressive educators, which brought into the educational bureaucracy educational ideas and practices that were not available within the state administration. Some of the progressive education circles in South India that influenced ABL's approach had adopted educational ideas of Indian philosopher J. Krishnamurti, while others were influenced by the Montessori method (as it turns out, Maria Montessori had spent many years in Madras, now Chennai – the capital of Tamil Nadu – and her ideas and methods had stayed alive in isolated pockets across southern India for generations). One of the most important influences for ABL was the Rishi Valley Institute for Educational Resources (RIVER), an NGO in the neighbouring state of Andhra Pradesh. It is from materials created by RIVER that teachers in Tamil Nadu first developed ABL. Furthermore, RIVER played an important role in the training of teachers from Tamil Nadu, and consulting on the development of ABL.

ABL started as a smaller pilot in the capital city of Chennai, and then spread across the state through a state-administered organization called *Sarva Shiksha Abhiyan* (SSA), India's flagship programme to universalize elementary education. In the early 2000s, MP Vijayakumar, then director of the SSA in Tamil Nadu, strategically placed prominent members of the network movement he helped brew over decades in key roles within the organization to shape teacher preparation, develop learning materials, and take on other responsibilities associated to spreading ABL across the state. Other network members supported the spread of ABL through consultancies and other informal roles. Throughout the widespread dissemination of ABL across Tamil Nadu, the central leadership was very intentional about working alongside teachers in a respectful and collaborative fashion. Additionally, Mr Vijayakumar and his team worked within the state's bureaucracy to enable the existence of ABL. They constantly travelled across the state to communicate their vision for education in Tamil Nadu, emphasize the centrality of student learning, address questions and doubts from teachers and administrators, and gain new supporters. They also worked to remove administrative roadblocks and deflect opposition.

Behind the rapid and widespread dissemination of ABL to thousands of government schools, one should also consider Tamil Nadu's century-long history of anti-caste political movements that developed in opposition to the belief in castes and the dominance of one caste over others, such as the Self-Respect Movement in the first half of the 1900s and the Dravida Munnetra Kazhagam (DMK), a political party created in the 1960s to oppose caste hierarchy and advance equity across all villages in the state. Together with its splinter, Anna DMK, this party has held power in Tamil Nadu since 1967, making this party's ideology a mainstay in Tamil Nadu. Embedded in ABL's pedagogy is a profound respect for children as autonomous and responsible learners, regardless of caste or religion, a conception that fits well in a state where the idea of castes has been challenged for over a century.

Throughout the book, I will sometimes draw on examples from the Global South more so than North America. I have decided to do this for several reasons. First, the most prominent examples of widespread pedagogical change available to date come from this region. Second, there are already enough ideas out there about educational change in high performing educational systems in the so called "developed" world – Canada, Finland, Japan, Singapore, and so on. And, third, a lot can be learned from the Global South if our purpose is not simply to emulate educational systems currently considered as high performing, but to reimagine and reinvent schools and school systems in order to turn them into vibrant places for learning and living examples of the societies we aspire to become.

This chapter offered a glimpse into liberating learning as can be observed in some – although still proportionally few – classrooms, schools, districts, and educational systems around the world. The portrayals just presented are consistent with what we know about how people and organizations learn best. Learning environments and systems such as the ones just described leverage on and feed the four key drivers of human motivation: mastery, purpose, autonomy, and connectedness.[6]

Against the Grain of Conventional Schooling

In many ways, liberating learning is easy to identify and relatively simple in its basic principles. At the same time, it is fundamentally different from conventional schooling. And decades of research on reform implementation make it clear that the default culture of schooling – both in schools and in school systems – is highly resilient, always ready to neutralize any serious effort to transform it.

Because of its inherently countercultural nature, liberating learning in classrooms, schools, and school systems requires hard work and deliberate efforts at identifying, navigating, and resolving the inevitable tensions that arise when the practices and mindsets required to liberate learning make their way into schools. In classrooms and schools that have succeeded at liberating learning as part of their regular practice, the initial efforts are often started by educators, school leaders, and sometimes students, who are ready to embrace and try out fundamentally different ways of working. Some strategies to liberate learning in schools include:

- Establishing a clear vision of what students are expected to learn and be able to do.
- Reorganizing the school schedule to secure extended blocks of time for deep immersion in learning.
- Creating time and space for teacher collaboration centred on examining and changing pedagogical practices to enhance student learning.
- Creating venues to discuss with parents about the new direction taken by the school.

But the most powerful force to liberate learning comes from experiencing powerful learning and witnessing visible and drastic improvements in student learning and engagement as a result of fundamentally transforming classroom practice. The testimonies of other teachers who have experienced the liberating power of learning are an effective vehicle to spread it to new sites. Encouraging visits to classrooms where learning has been unleashed, as well as facilitating constant informal communication between teachers who embrace this work and less enthusiastic teachers can be useful tactics to liberate learning in new classrooms. The enthusiasm generated by experiencing and witnessing powerful learning creates a tremendous force to change the default culture of schooling.

Connecting with other schools invested in liberating learning is also helpful to advance its widespread dissemination It fosters a sense of collective identity around a compelling agenda and creates opportunities for schools to learn from one another. Indeed, many of the schools that have been identified as exemplars of deeper learning belong to networks of schools committed to this agenda.[7]

Developing networks of schools invested in liberating learning also creates collective power, which increases the chances of successfully negotiating with system administrators to secure political and administrative support to liberate learning and ensure its sustainability. Some school networks that embrace learner-centred pedagogics, for example, have secured waivers from the testing regime in their State, using instead student portfolios and comprehensive performance review panels to grant high school completion degrees to their students (see for example Grossman, 2010).

In the next chapter, I will present and discuss the theoretical foundations upon which the ideas in this book are built.

Notes

1 This vignette draws from a case study prepared by Michael Fullan and his team for the Ministry of Education in Ontario (Fullan, Rodway, & Rincón-Gallardo, 2016).
2 The Ottawa Catholic School Board and its work to deepen student learning across the entire system is featured in *Deep Learning: Engage the World, Change the World* (Fullan, Quinn, & McEachen, 2017). The vignette presented here draws on this work, as well as on an earlier case study developed by Michael Fullan and his team (Fullan, Rincón-Gallardo, & Rodway, 2017).
3 More detailed information about the history, strategy, and results of the Learning Community Project (Tutorial Networks) in Mexico can be found in Rincón-Gallardo (2016) and Rincón-Gallardo and Elmore (2012).
4 For a good window into Escuela Nueva, the reader can review the work of Vicky Colbert and Jairo Arboleda (Colbert & Arboleda, 2016), Alfredo Sarmiento and Vicky Colbert (Sarmiento & Colbert, 2018), and Ernesto Schiefelbein (1993).
5 The most comprehensive accounts of the history and development of the Activity Based Learning model in Tamil Nadu are to be found in the work of Tricia Niesz Ramchandar Krishnamurthy (2013, 2014) and Ryan (2018).
6 These four drivers of intrinsic motivation are extracted from Edward L. Deci and Richard M. Ryan's Self Determination Theory (Deci & Ryan, 2000) and Daniel Pink's (2011) *Drive*. The three determinants of intrinsic motivation in Deci and Ryan's Self Determination Theory are Autonomy, Competence (which I refer to as Mastery), and Relatedness (which I refer to as Connectedness). Pink's three drivers of intrinsic motivation are Purpose, Mastery, and Autonomy.
7 Some of these school networks include High Tech High, NuVu, Big Picture Schools, New Tech Network International Network for Public Schools, New Pedagogies for Deep Learning, Envision Education, EdVisions Schools, and EL Schools.

3

EDUCATIONAL CHANGE AS SOCIAL MOVEMENT

Turning public education into a deliberate and effective vehicle to prepare our younger generations to be confident learners and compassionate citizens calls for a cultural shift of massive proportions. Schooling has historically played three core functions: custody, control, and distribution of merit. Its structures and institutional processes are organized in the service of these functions. Student learning and active citizenship may be prioritized in public discourses and official documents. In practice, however, the institutional culture and conventional power relationships of schooling often end up interfering with the realization of these higher goals.

Learning and active citizenship are acts of freedom, triggered by people's determination to pursue questions and issues that matter to them. Active learners and citizens often experience *flow*, a deeply fulfilling state of maximum absorption and concentration, in which the sense of time and consciousness of self disappears. In other words, both are fuelled by intrinsic motivation.

Contrast this with the experiences afforded to most children and youth attending conventional school: each day organized into timed sessions during which pre-determined content is presented to the whole group with the expectation that everybody will learn, at the same time and pace. Test scores are the main measure of success, while sitting and listening quietly are valued as the appropriate behaviour.

As Daniel Pink (2009) points out in his book, *Drive: The Surprising Truth about What Motivates Us*, schools, as many other organizations in contemporary societies, were designed under assumptions about human motivation that contrast with more recent knowledge about human behaviour. The dominant "operating system" of many schools and workplaces assumes that work is boring and unfulfilling, and for this reason it has to be shaped through extrinsic motivators (grades, test scores and teacher approval, et cetera) The *carrots-and-sticks* approach is effective for a range of routine tasks, but these are disappearing from human work with the rise of robots and automatization. And they are far from the rich, complex work that characterizes liberating learning. Indeed, rewards and punishments even work against their intended purpose, by decreasing internal motivation and crushing creativity.

Complex and unpredictable in nature, liberating learning requires what Pink (2009) calls a new "operating system", built around intrinsic motivation, which involves:

- purpose (having a clear end in mind and connecting what we do to something larger than ourselves);
- mastery (getting better at what we do);
- autonomy (having the freedom to determine what we do, as well as when, how, and with whom we do it);
- connectedness (working in connection with others).

Looking at schooling through the lens of these four elements reveals that many schools and school systems urgently need a new operating system.

Some schools do cultivate the skills and mindsets required for learning and citizenship, while some high-performing networks offer lessons about improving teaching and learning at scale. However, such successes are relatively rare. Since the emergence of compulsory schooling, committed educators around the world have created classrooms and schools that leverage and fuel intrinsic motivation, liberating learning among children and youth. These include schools and school networks such as Montessori schools and Waldorf schools, Reggio Emilia in Italy, Freedom Schools in the English-speaking world, High Tech High in California and Democratic Schools around the globe, among others. But these remain isolated examples, led by a handful of committed educators and leaders who often turn inwards to create their bubbles of freedom. They do this while leaving the rest of the system intact.

It is also possible to find high-performing systems that appear to be quite successful at scale. For the past two decades, since the launch of the Programme for International Student Assessment (PISA) of the Organisation for Economic Cooperation and Development (OECD), a rich body of international and comparative research has emerged, aimed at understanding how high-performing systems around the world have achieved their success.[1] This work shows the value of paying attention to: equity (closing the gap in educational opportunity between "vulnerable" and privileged students), the professional growth of educators, and aligning the organization of the system around ambitious goals for student learning. Many of these lessons will apply in the new systems required to liberate learning.

But these lessons offer an incomplete picture of what will be required. High system performance is, for the most part, successful operation of conventional schooling and its basic operating system, fostering performance through extrinsic incentives, with learning that can be measured through standardized tests. A few exceptions, such as Finland and Ontario, have achieved their success in international standardized tests without paying much mind to improving test scores. These systems have started to shift their logic of operation to one that is more consistent with the logic that will be required in the education systems of the future. But even these systems are far from fully operating as organizations focused on liberating learning. We are yet to see large numbers of schools and entire educational systems deliberately cultivating purpose, autonomy, mastery, and connectedness. Creating education systems that fully embrace and set in motion a liberating learning agenda will require that we open up the "black box" of human learning and fundamentally reconfigure how we think about and carry on education practice and policy.

Opening up the black box will mean a massive cultural shift, a radical departure from what we have come to understand and value as learning, teaching, achievement, assessment, and management. Throughout history, the most effective agents of widespread cultural change – and in particular, cultural change that moves us closer to our human condition – have been social movements. Social movements offer a powerful metaphor for the new paradigm to guide how we think about and pursue educational change.

Of course, social movements are not always inherently virtuous; some advance ideologies grounded on hatred and intolerance. My intention is not to idealize social movements, but to identify in their logic of operation a useful metaphor to redefine how we think about educational change while advancing a "cause" – liberating learning – that can bring us closer to our shared humanity.

Good Bye, Scientific Management, Hello Social Movements

Paradigms are ways to explain the world that define not only how we think but also how we act in the world. Scientific management, the paradigm that has shaped thought and action in schools since the establishment of compulsory schooling, provides a powerful metaphor to design and manage schools and educational systems. First developed by Frederick Taylor in the wake of the industrial revolution, scientific management breaks down human activity into repetitive routine tasks and introduces external incentives to ensure adequate implementation.

In education, the ideas of scientific management (standards, testing, and accountability) have shaped education reform for the past century. In his discussion of the powerful influence that paradigms have on politics, Mehta (2013, p. 23) explains that

> once crystallized, a new paradigm not only delimits policy options to conform to that paradigm, but restructures the political landscape around an issue, raises the agenda status of the issue, and changes the players involved, their standing to speak, and the venue in which the issue is debated.

Standards, testing, and accountability have powerfully shaped education policy in the United States for decades. The idea that system-wide school improvement is best achieved by rationalizing school activities through principles of scientific management took a strong hold and continues to be the dominant paradigm for education reform in the United States, also pervading education reforms in many other countries.

The paradigm has had tremendous appeal for politicians across the political spectrum, as well as for system leaders and other education stakeholders. For liberals, standards and school accountability appeal for their promise of greater equity and consistency of educational services. For conservatives, the appeal lies in the promise of efficient spending of public money. For advocacy groups and administrators, standards and accountability promise to bring order to an unwieldly system, and focus it on improved outcomes.

Alluring as standards, testing, and accountability are, their main drawback lies in their failure to produce the intended results. Michael Fullan (2011) has framed the problem as "choosing the wrong drivers for whole system reform". Drivers are policies or approaches to educational change intended to cause improved student outcomes. Wrong drivers do not produce their intended results. These are: external accountability, technology, individualistic solutions, and ad hoc strategies. Right drivers, on the other hand, have proved effective in improving student learning outcomes. They are: capacity building, pedagogy, collaboration, and "systemness" (that is, solutions aimed at affecting the whole system, or big chunks of it). Unfortunately, pursuing the wrong drivers is relatively easy: they can be legislated, stated simply and clearly, and appeal to the larger public. In contrast, the right drivers are relatively vague and have to be developed. For this reason, right drivers often have less public appeal.

Pursuing the right drivers requires clarity and specificity about what they look like in practice along with the conditions to enable their diffusion across entire educational systems. But that is not enough. If right drivers are used within organizations that operate within the logic of scientific management, their effectiveness will be limited. To reap the power of the right drivers, a new paradigm for educational change is necessary. The idea of *educational change as a social movement* offers a good metaphor for such a new paradigm.

While scientific management relies on control and compliance, social movements rely on autonomy and creativity. In scientific management, leadership is hierarchical in nature, whereas in social movements it is distributed. Scientific management strives for achievement and efficiency, while social movements prioritize learning and efficacy. Scientific management operates through prescription, mandates, and external accountability, whereas the modus operandi of social movements involves dialogue, deliberation, and internal accountability. Scientific management relies for its success on external accountability and resources, whereas social movements depend on intrinsic motivation and resourcefulness. Scientific management strives for stability, social movements pursue cultural renewal. Scientific management approaches change incrementally. Social movements are revolutionary forces of change.

TABLE 3.1. Scientific Management vs Social Movement

	Scientific Management	Social Movement
Leadership	Control/compliance Hierarchical	Autonomy/creativity Networked, distributed
Core values	Achievement Efficiency	Learning Efficacy
Core practices	Prescription Mandates External accountability	Dialogue Deliberation Internal accountability
Relies on	External incentives Resources	Intrinsic motivation Resourcefulness
Stance on change	Stability Incrementalism	Cultural renewal Radical innovation

Four Attempts to Override Scientific Management

The scientific management paradigm has proven to be remarkably resilient, surviving unscathed in spite of four sets of ideas that might have been expected to at least diminish its appeal (see Table 3.2). These four sets of ideas are:

1. Progressive education and critical pedagogy.
2. Teacher professionalism.
3. Sense-making/co-construction.
4. Organic view of educational systems.

TABLE 3.2. Merits and Shortcomings of Four Attempts to Override Scientific Management

	Merits	Shortcomings
Progressive education + critical pedagogy	Focus on student learning and democracy Critique of conventional schooling	Isolated examples Failure to become the new "normal"
Teacher professionalism	Call for turning teaching into fully-fledged profession Transfer of power and authority to educators	Failure to appeal to/include wider sectors of society Silent re: learning for the future and democracy
Sense-making/co-construction	More adequate explanation of policy implementation and educational change	Silent re: purpose of educational change Equally fit to maintain or change the status quo
Organic view of educational systems	Appealing metaphor of systems that operate in accordance to human nature and life	Silent re: power and how to confront and redefine it

The first set of ideas standing in tension with the dominant paradigm is represented by *progressive education and critical pedagogy*. Since the early decades of the twentieth century, prominent education thinkers such as John Dewey, Maria Montessori, and Jean Piaget dedicated much of their work and thought to developing theory and practical knowledge on how children learn. Progressive educators focused on designing pedagogies and learning environments best suited to cultivate the natural inclination and capacity of children and youth to learn. The progressive education tradition has continued to grow through educators and thinkers such as Eleanor Duckworth, Howard Gardner, and David Perkins.

Critical pedagogy, with origins in the work of Paulo Freire, rejects the notion of neutrality of knowledge and insists that the pursuit of social justice and democracy should not be separate from the practice of teaching and learning. More contemporary proponents of critical pedagogy include Jeff Duncan-Andrade, Henry Giroux, Gloria Ladson-Billings, bell hooks, and Peter McLaren. Adopting and developing concepts from critical theory and cultural studies, critical pedagogy sees education, and the practice of teaching, as inherently political. Proponents of critical pedagogy see learning as *praxis*, a process of acting and reflecting on the world that awakens critical consciousness and leads to emancipation from oppression.

All along, progressive educators and advocates of critical pedagogy have criticized conventional schooling. While progressive educators criticize the standardization of conventional schooling as inadequate and harmful to the innate desire and capacity of children to learn, proponents of critical pedagogy highlight the oppressive function of schooling, its neglect of the contexts in which the lives of students unfold, and the authoritarian nature of conventional teaching. Both progressive education and critical pedagogy have developed a base of knowledge about the nature of learning and the best conditions for it to thrive. Both have articulated critiques to the inadequacy of conventional schooling to produce liberating learning and robust democracies. The two fields have inspired the creation of individual classrooms and schools that are living examples of progressive education or emancipatory praxis.

The major shortcoming of these two traditions as models for education reform lies in their failure to become the new normal across entire education systems. Schools such as Reggio-Emilia, Montessori, Waldorf, Democratic Schools, and Free Schools continue to be relatively isolated bubbles of hope in the midst of a remarkably unchanged schooling landscape. A new paradigm should leverage the rich tradition of progressive education and critical pedagogy for insights on the nature of learning and the practices that help it thrive. At the same time, a successful paradigm must stimulate the transformation of entire educational systems. In other words, a new paradigm should offer solutions at both the micro-levels of classroom practice and school organization and at the macro-levels of policy development and organizational management.

Teacher professionalism represents a second set of ideas to counterbalance the paradigm of scientific management in education. Teacher professionalism proponents argue that improving schools and school systems requires the recognition and organization of teaching as a full-fledged profession.[2] They point to several crucial features of professionalism: 1) a solid knowledge base that practitioners are expected to master; 2) shared norms and standards of practice; and 3) the power and authority to define who can become a certified practitioner or a licensed provider of training for future members of the profession. Some jurisdictions have made progress in these areas, particularly through establishing self-governing professional bodies. Over the past couple of decades, calls for teachers' control of their own professional practice have often focused on the development and power of collaborative cultures (within schools, between schools, and between school systems) to improve instructional practice, change the culture of schools, and develop more coherent systems.[3]

Teacher professionalism has not provided a viable alternative to the scientific management paradigm and seems unlikely to do so. The pursuit of a full-fledged independent teaching profession might be appealing to some educators and progressive education leaders, but it has failed to gain the support of wider sectors of society. Some advocacy and community organizing groups are likely to see in the devolution of authority over curriculum, instruction, and school management to teachers as undermining the power of parents and communities to hold teachers and schools accountable for the education delivered to young people. Furthermore, granting teachers full authority and control over the profession would run the risk of pushing other important actors aside (e.g. parents, students, and society at large), and exclude worldviews, cultures, and ways of knowing that do not conform to the dominant set of beliefs about what constitutes valid knowledge and skills.

Teacher professionalism does not address two key problems for the future of education. The first is the need to redefine what students should know and be able to do as a result of going to school, in response to the massive economic, environmental, and societal shifts of this century. The definition of twenty-first century knowledge and skills should involve a wide range of sectors of society, of which the teaching profession is only one. The second unaddressed issue is the pursuit of democracy as an explicit goal of formal education. It is not clear whether and how a full-fledged teaching profession would contribute to the construction of robust democracies. Teacher professionalism will be an important aspect of renewing public education, but it is not sufficient to become the new paradigm for educational change.

A third prominent set of ideas relates to educational change, more specifically a *sense-making/co-construction* perspective on education reform. In the wake of the 1980s, Paul Berman (1981) argued that school change was an implementation-dominant, not a technological-dominant process – that is, what determines the fate of education reform is not its design, but what those expected to implement it do with it. Ten years later, in his classic book, *The Meaning of Educational Change*, Michael Fullan (1991) pointed out that neglect of the phenomenology of change – that is, how people on the ground make sense of education policy, as opposed to how it is expected by policy makers – was at the heart of the spectacular lack of success of most education reform efforts. Since then, and aligned with such thinking, a robust body of research explored the meanings that teachers made of education reforms and how their interpretations influenced the implementation of policy changes. This research provides compelling evidence that teachers' responses to reform are influenced by their understandings of policy messages, which are in turn shaped by teacher beliefs and experiences, and the contexts in which they try to make sense of policy. In the last decade, Amanda Datnow and Vicki Park proposed a "sense-making/co-construction" perspective for policy implementation (Datnow & Park, 2009). Under this perspective, education policy is conceptualized as an iterative and complex process that requires the active participation and interaction between multiple actors and contexts.

The *sense-making/co-construction* perspective offers a more nuanced explanation for the development and implementation of educational change than does the technical-rational perspective (inspired by principles of scientific management), which assumes that education policy flows through a direct line from central offices to classrooms. As well, this perspective can apply to a wide range of processes of education policy development and implementation, regardless of their focus (e.g. curriculum or instructional improvement) or their locus of development (e.g. central governing body or grassroots level).

However, the *sense-making/co-construction perspective* is insufficient to respond to two key questions in need of attention for the future of educational change. The perspective is silent on the question of purpose. And it leaves the question of whether a specific educational change endeavour perpetuates or subverts the status quo unanswered.

The fourth and final set of ideas attempting to define a new paradigm for educational change adopts notions of *organic systems* as metaphors for the type of educational systems needed for the future.[4] The metaphor of educational systems as living environments that operate in consonance with the natural flow of human life is in stark contrast with the images of machines and factories inspired by scientific management. This alternative image offers an appealing metaphor for the school systems of the future.

The main shortcoming of this organic view of educational systems is that it does not provide a roadmap to realize it. It does not account for the pervasive nature of the default culture schooling, and fails to provide a set of strategies or principles of action to confront and fundamentally change the dominant patterns of authority and control of conventional schools and school systems. Said differently, an organic view of educational systems pays little attention to how to change the default culture of schools and school systems.

The four sets of ideas just described – progressive education and critical pedagogy, teacher professionalism, the sense-making/co-construction perspective on educational change, and the organic view of educational systems – have sought to critique and propose alternatives to the scientific management paradigm. Individually and by themselves, however, they are not conceptually powerful enough to overturn the dominant paradigm and establish a new paradigm for educational change.

As I have suggested, *educational change as social movement* offers an appealing metaphor for the new paradigm. On the one hand, it is compatible with the most important contributions of the four sets of ideas just discussed. On the other, it addresses several of their shortcomings. While grounded on the philosophy and practice of progressive education and critical pedagogy, *educational change as social movement* offers a theory of action to transform entire educational systems, rather than just individual schools. It embraces and acknowledges the fundamental role of a full-fledged teaching profession while, at the same time, it includes and is likely to appeal to a much wider range of actors, including students and advocacy and community organizing groups. It builds on the notion that educational change is a complex, multi-directional phenomenon shaped by the agency of all actors involved, while offering a specific, compelling purpose for educational change and deliberately seeking to fundamentally change the culture of schooling. It embraces the vision of schools and school systems that are more attuned to our human nature, while offering a set of principles of action to confront and redefine the default institutional culture and power relationships of schooling in classrooms, schools, and educational systems.

The New Paradigm Emerging in the Global South

Paradigm shifts occur as scientific revolutions, rather than through incremental additions to existing knowledge (Kuhn, 1970). They usually start with the emergence of "anomalies" that contradict the existing paradigm or that cannot be explained by such paradigms. New paradigms reconstruct prior assumptions and re-evaluate prior facts in ways that integrate "anomalies" into coherent explanations on how the world works. When a paradigm shift takes place a community of knowledge starts to think about and act on the world in an entirely different way. In education, there are currently signs suggesting that the prevalence of scientific management as the dominant paradigm for educational change is coming to an end, along with indications that *educational change as social movement* has some good chances to supplant it as the new paradigm.

Scientific management, the dominant paradigm in education policy and practice, is based on the idea that the most effective way to run an organization is to break down complex work into simple, repetitive tasks, and create external incentives to secure adequate execution. Over four decades of policy implementation, studies have demonstrated that scientific management is inadequate as an explanation or driver of educational change. "Anomalies" to the scientific management paradigm are increasingly obvious.

The Global South offers a rich source of "anomalies" of another sort. These "anomalies" are examples of successful widespread pedagogical change that defy the dominant paradigm. These are examples of fundamentally changing the pedagogical core in schools serving historically marginalized communities, doing it at scale (hundreds or thousands of schools), and achieving measurable improvements in student outcomes, at a faster pace and sometimes surpassing the achievement of schools serving more privileged students. I'm talking about the Learning Community Project (LCP, also known as Tutorial Networks) in Mexico (Rincón-Gallardo & Elmore, 2012; Rincón-Gallardo, 2016), Escuela Nueva in Colombia (Colbert & Arboleda, 2016; Schiefelbein, 1993), the Activity Based Learning model in the Southern State of Tamil Nadu in India (Niesz & Krishnamurthy, 2013, 2014), and Community Schools in Northern Egypt (Zaalouk, 2006).

These four cases developed independently from one another. And yet, they share several features in common, including:

- focus on child-centred pedagogies;
- emphasis on serving remote and historically marginalized communities;
- roots in local culture and history;
- emergence as grassroots efforts evolving into large-scale policies, with access to institutional power to maintain the "spirit" of the change;
- deliberate efforts to change relationship between central leadership and schools; and
- success in improving student outcomes, even though raising standard measures was not a central aspect of the strategies.

What makes these examples "anomalies"? They defy conventional definitions of education policy. They are more similar in their genesis and development to social movements. (Indeed, these four cases have been described as social movements, at different moments in time, by different scholars who were not aware of each other's work.) They advance fundamental changes in dominant patters of social interaction (between young people and adults, and between policy and practice). They rely on voluntary participation and resourcefulness – learning to turn what they have into what they need to get what they want. And they build collective capacity to mobilize and change what gets in the way of their change efforts.

Under the dominant paradigm, relationships within the pedagogical core and between policy and practice are hierarchical in nature. In the new paradigm, these relationships are more horizontal, grounded on dialogue, co-learning, and mutual influence. These new sets of relationships, as I argued earlier, are better suited for learning and more adequate to nurture the habits of thought and action required in robust democracies.

Educational change has to be about cultural renewal that zeroes-in on liberating learning. Throughout history, social movements have served as the most powerful collective agents of cultural change. In their ways of operating lie important clues to redefining how young people and adults interact with each other in schools, and how administrators and educators interact with each other in educational systems. What's perhaps most important, the idea of *educational change as social movement* is not simply a theoretical approach, but rather emerges from efforts to explain existing examples of widespread pedagogical change that do not fit the dominant paradigm.

For the remainder of this chapter, I will define the key concepts underpinning the ideas presented throughout the book. I see large-scale pedagogical transformation as a phenomenon of widespread cultural change. Inspired by Thomas Rochon's (1998) work, I posit that widespread cultural change in classrooms, schools, and education systems occurs when new educational values and practices developed by a critical community are taken up by movements that spread them in three arenas: the pedagogical, the social, and the political arenas. I will first offer working definitions of core concepts such as learning, pedagogy, culture, counterculture, scale, cultural change, and social movements. I will then bring these concepts together to define and further unpack the idea of educational change as social movement.

Learning, Pedagogy, Culture, and Scale

Learning: A Practice of Freedom

Student learning has remained a marginal area of concern for the educational change field, in spite of statements to the contrary. The field has been built on simplistic, imperfect, and partial proxies for the complex phenomenon of learning – e.g. student achievement scores in standardized tests, course completion, attainment of credentials, and graduation rates. Furthermore, learning – or more specifically its very imperfect proxy of student achievement – has been overwhelmingly seen and valued for its individualistic and utilitarian functions. For example, scores in standardized tests are seen as indicators of preparedness for future employability or as measures of college readiness, while high-school certificates are valued as requisites to enter college. Such narrow vision perpetuates a view of learning as a commodity to be attained for better individual economic benefits or as preparation to enter the work force. This perspective offers an important but dangerously incomplete view of learning, with important implications for the prospect of nurturing robust democracies. Thinking about and acting on a commoditized vision of learning while omitting its more holistic nature and its liberating function can cultivate cadres of young people who are compliant, obedient, and passive, no matter how grandiloquent and lofty the aspirations of schools and education systems.

So, what do I mean by learning? Learning is a process and the result of making sense of questions that matter to us (Rogers, 1969). It involves using what we already know and know how to do to make meaning of new concepts and ideas, solve new problems, or master new skills – a phenomenon that has come to be known as *transfer* (Bellanca, 2015). Learning is both cognitive and emotional, often involving stages such as the excitement of exploring an intriguing question, the anxiety that comes from struggling to find clarity, and the exhilaration of understanding what was at first confusing. Despite being a mysterious and complex phenomenon, learning is something we as humans are wired to do with ease *given the right conditions.*

Intrinsic motivation is fundamental for learning – or at least for learning that is worthwhile and has staying power. We learn well only what we are interested in learning. Or said differently, without interest, there is no lasting, worthwhile learning. When an idea, a procedure, or a lesson is imposed on us through external incentives, we might be able to memorize it for a short period of time, even get an excellent grade in a test, but its lasting power, and its relevance to our lives, is minimal. Consider the following example, reported in the documentary film *Most Likely to Succeed.* [5] Students were asked to retake a final science exam three months after completing the course. The second time around, all low-level details of the previous test were removed. The first time the students took the test, the average grade was B+. After only three months, the average grade of the group – the same students, taking the same although simpler test – dropped to F! No students still had command of the major science concepts they presumably "mastered" only three months earlier!

Recent discoveries of cognitive science are consistent with this report. As Linda Darling Hammond reports in the same film, *inert knowledge* – that is, knowledge that you memorize for a test, put it on paper the next day and don't use – disappears about 90 per cent of the time. Inert knowledge does not stick. Looking with honesty at our own schooling experiences, the results reported in the film should come as no surprise. After all, how would you fare if you were to take right now a test you took and passed when you were in high school? Or how much of the curriculum you were taught at school do you use or remember?

If intrinsic motivation is a pre-condition for learning, what are the essential features of work that's intrinsically motivating? As I mentioned earlier in this chapter, there are four key drivers of intrinsic motivation: purpose, mastery, autonomy, and connectedness. These four drivers offer a useful framework to understand the nature of the tasks and conditions likely to stimulate learning. Looked at through the lens of these four drivers, schooling appears as a less than ideal – if not a disabling – technology for intrinsic motivation and particularly for learning.

In this section, I have talked about learning as a fundamentally human activity that extends beyond its mere individualistic or utilitarian purposes and beyond its merely cognitive dimensions. I have also pointed out the crucial role that intrinsic motivation plays in fostering learning.

Conditions for learning: Constant Exposure, Constant Practice, Constant Feedback

What are key conditions that help us learn deeply? I sum it up in three major conditions: constant exposure, constant practice, and constant feedback. Learning any complex activity, whether playing a sport, playing a musical instrument, speaking a new language, or doing scientific inquiry, involves a similar process and similar enabling conditions. The first is constant exposure, in real time, to the expert practice we want to learn, performed by experts – sport players, an accomplished music player, native speakers of a language, or scientists. The second is multiple opportunities to try out and refine the practice by fully taking part in it, be it practising a sport, playing a musical instrument, speaking a new language, or doing scientific inquiry. And the third is abundant and constant sources of feedback. This includes, for example, whether your actions while playing a sport helped or hindered your team's success, the sounds produced by your attempts to play an instrument; signs of whether and to what degree your interlocutor understood what you said in a new language; whether or not your inquiry led to a discovery, a new insight, or a breakthrough.

Conventional schooling as we know it falls short of creating these three conditions. Let's start with exposure. Arguably, learning to learn is one of the fundamental skills any school system expects to develop and nurture in young people. Almost any curriculum across the globe will include "learning to learn" as a key aspiration. Ironically, and in stark contrast with the examples of activities discussed in the previous paragraph, *the practice of learning* remains for the most part invisible for students. As a practice, learning is something educators do privately when preparing their lessons, and something that students are expected to do when doing homework or preparing for an exam. That is, the practice of learning is relegated to the private realm. And this negates the possibility of young people getting constant exposure to learning as a practice. With little access and attention to learning as a practice, the other two conditions to get better – deliberate practice and constant feedback – remain, for the most part, absent in the everyday lives of classrooms and schools.

Pedagogy: I, Thou, and It

The term pedagogy refers to the practice of supporting someone else's learning, together with the guiding principles underlying such practice. More specifically, pedagogy refers to the dynamic relationship between an educator and a learner in the presence of knowledge, or the interactions that take place within the pedagogical core. Put in David Hawkins' (1974) words, a pedagogical relationship always involves an "I", a "Thou", and an "It" – that is, two (or more) people and an object of knowledge that brings them together in a common pursuit of meaning.

I have chosen the term "pedagogy" over "instruction" for several reasons. First, the term instruction tends to emphasize the technical and instrumental dimensions of the practice of teaching. On the technical side, aspects such as the time spent on a task or the structuring of a lesson are given prominent attention. On the instrumental side, instructional change is advocated for mostly on the grounds of its expected positive effects on student outcomes (Doyle, 1983; Hattie, 2009). Important as these aspects of educational practice are, however, they tend to overlook or flat out neglect its political dimensions.

The pedagogical core is not only the basic unit where learning happens – or not – but also a basic unit of social relationships of power and authority. From this perspective, educational practice should be looked at not only for its effects on conventional student outcomes, but also for its role in perpetuating or subverting existing social relationships of authority and control. The term "pedagogy", as used for example in Paulo Freire's (1970) *Pedagogy of the Oppressed*, allows for an emphasis not only on the technical and instrumental dimensions of educational practice, but also its cultural and political dimensions.

Second, the term "instruction" implicitly establishes a vertical separation between the person who "instructs" (the teacher) and the person who is "instructed" (the student). The term pedagogy allows this type of hierarchical relationship: we could say, for example, that conventional teaching is an authoritarian form of pedagogy, but is also open to alternative arrangements – for example, peer-to-peer support, students as experts or teachers as learners.

Culture: The Operating System of Human Groups

Culture is the operating system of a human group. It consists of historically derived and selected ideas, beliefs, values, artefacts, practices and patterns of behaviour that constitute what is considered the "taken-for-granted" in a human group. Our actions create culture while, at the same time, they are shaped by it. Culture serves as an all-encompassing matrix of meaning in and through which societal values and practices as well relationships of power and authority are reproduced, but also challenged and transformed.[6] In this sense, culture is not a static, but a dynamic, phenomenon where forces of the status quo and forces of change are in constant interaction. Because it shapes and is shaped by relationships of power, culture is inherently political (Norton, 2004).

Several authors in the educational change field have used the French proverb *plus ça change, plus c'est la même chose* (the more things change the more they stay the same) to illustrate the pervasiveness and resiliency of what has come to be termed the default culture of schooling, the established instructional culture and institutional structure of schools (Elmore, 1996; Sarason, 1982). Some distinguishing features of such default culture include a top-down separation between teaching and learning, with authority and control concentrated in teachers; a focus on covering content at the same time and pace for the whole group; and a prioritization of covering content over ensuring student understanding.

Culture is inherently a conservative force. It exerts a powerful influence over the beliefs and behaviours of people to preserve continuity and oppose change (Evans, 1996). Culture can be powerful in ruling out options for change. The nature of culture as a conservative force is consistent no matter how compelling the necessity for change may seem from an external perspective. And with reason, as "no institution can readily abandon the deep structures on which its very coherence and significance depends" (Evans, 1996, p. 50).

Countercultural Practice: Against the Grain

A pedagogical principle or practice is countercultural when it fundamentally redefines the relationships within the pedagogical core; that is, when it redefines the established relationships between teachers and students in the presence of knowledge. I use the term counterculture as an adaptation from Antonio Gramsci's concepts of hegemony and counter-hegemony (Broccoli, 1979; Gramsci, 1971; Thomas, 2009) to deliberately position prospects of pedagogical change in the larger context of social relations of power, authority, and control. Broadly speaking, modern institutions – e.g. the medical establishment, schooling, the State – are characterized by vertical relationships of authority and control, with a hierarchical separation between experts – e.g., a doctor, a teacher, a politician – considered to have superior knowledge and whose role is to dictate what to do and how, and "aco-lytes" – the patient, the student, the citizen – whose role is to follow the indications of the authority. While often reproduced through the institution of schooling (see for example, Apple, 2004; Bourdieu & Passeron, 1977; Willis, 1977), dominant social relations may be subverted through the development of practices that establish new social relations based on more humanist principles of dialogue and respect.

Research on effective pedagogy provides important insight into the practices, principles, and conditions that enhance teacher and student learning. John Hattie, for instance, has conducted a comprehensive meta-analysis of classroom practices with the largest positive effects on student outcomes. These include: 1) Reci-procal teaching – that is, enabling students to self-direct their learning and to engage in peer-to-peer support; 2) Specific feedback to student work; 3) Pro-moting self-verbalization and self-questioning among students; 4) Metacognition, that is, cultivating in students the ability to reflect on their own thinking; and 5) Problem-solving. Taking his conclusions one step further, Hattie (2009, p. 25) suggests that

> what is most important is that teaching is visible to the student and that learning is visible to the teacher. The more the student becomes the teacher and the more the teacher becomes the learner then the more successful are the outcomes.

Liberating learning requires that we move away from conventional pedagogies built around extrinsic motivation and instead advance pedagogies that leverage and feed purpose, autonomy, mastery, and connectedness. It requires a fundamental shift in the nature of the relationship between teachers and students in the presence of knowledge: from vertical relationships of authority and control to horizontal relationships of mutual learning and dialogue. This is, inherently, countercultural work.

Scale: From Few to Many

Spreading new pedagogical practices to large numbers of sites or across an entire educational system is a process of *widespread cultural change*. In stating this, I depart from the technical-rational paradigm under which the term of scale was originally conceived. From a technical-rational perspective, scale is merely the number of actors or sites adopting an intervention, and the process of scaling is understood as replication of an intervention in multiple sites (Glennan, Bodilly, Galegher, & Kerr, 2004).

The notion of large-scale pedagogical transformation as widespread cultural change encompasses four main ideas:

- changing pedagogy as a cultural project;
- importance of transforming the pedagogical core;
- disruption of social relations of power, authority, and control;
- establishing new social relations.

First, the problem of changing pedagogy at scale is seen not only as a technical but, more importantly, a cultural project. Several authors in the educational change field have observed how profoundly resilient the default culture of schooling is to any attempts to transform it. This resilience persists in spite of key defining features of the default culture being at odds with how children learn best and the teaching practices that most improve student learning. Consequently, effective pedagogical change requires the disruption of the default culture of schooling and the creation of a new culture that enables deeper student learning.

Second, the pedagogical core is the fundamental unit where large-scale pedagogical change has to occur. Disrupting the default culture of schooling involves changing in fundamental ways the nature of the relationships within the pedagogical core.

Third is the deliberate positioning of prospects of pedagogical change in the context of social relations of power, authority, and control. Historically, there has been a clear hierarchical divide between teachers and students in classrooms, and between education policy and teachers: teachers over students, policy over practice. Since relationships of power are inherent to classroom practice and education policy, they are political (Freire, 1970).

And, fourth, "cultural change" is understood here not only as one that disrupts or subverts dominant social relations in classrooms and in policy making, but one that deliberately seeks to establish new social relations based on humanist principles of dialogue, respect, partnership, and solidarity (Freire, 1970; hooks, 1994).

Social Movements and Educational Change

Social movements are collective agents of cultural and political transformation. They

> emerge as a result of the efforts of purposeful actors (individuals, organizations) to assert new public values, form new relationships rooted in those values, and mobilize the political, economic, and cultural power to translate these values into action. They differ from fashions, styles or fads […] in that they are collective, strategic, and organized […] They differ from interest groups in that they focus […] not only winning the game, but also changing the rules.
>
> *(Ganz, 2010, p. 1)*

Despite their key role as vehicles of cultural transformation, the countercultural work of social movements has remained mostly unexamined. And despite being qualitatively distinct from interest groups, social movements have been studied mainly as rational collective actors pursuing instrumental goals in the institutional or political arenas. A review of contemporary social movements identifies three broad sets of factors to explain the emergence and development of social movements: political opportunities, mobilizing structures, and framing (McAdam, McCarthey, & Zald, 1996; Tarrow, 2011). *Political opportunities* refer to the broader set of political constraints and circumstances that shape social movements. *Mobilizing structures* are the collective vehicles – both formal and informal – through which social movement actors engage in collective action. *Framing processes* refer to the ways in which social movements create narratives to attract supporters and deflect opposition.

Important as these three sets of factors are to explain how social movements emerge and develop, they offer incomplete accounts of social movements in that they overlook individual and collective agency. As Ganz (2010) points out, research on social movements, with a few exceptions, has a strong structural bias, focusing more on the constraining conditions than on the enabling conditions that could make many outcomes possible. Ganz poignantly observes that agency, understood as choice in the face of uncertainty "is more about grasping at possibility than conforming to probability" (p. 2). My focus is on the role of social movements as collective agents of cultural change, and on the individual and collective agency that brings social movements to life and sustains them over the long run.

Not all social movements support virtuous change – either in the causes they pursue or the means used to pursue them. My purview throughout this book is limited to non-extremist movements that advance humanistic principles of equity, solidarity, and collective freedom. My focus is on the logic of operation of these movements, examining their evocative power to liberate learning in schools and across entire educational systems.

In understanding social movements and educational change, Tricia Niesz and her colleagues at Kent State University (Niesz, Korora, Burke Walkuski, & Foot, 2018)[7] identified two broad categories in a review of over 350 studies. The first category, primarily in adult education, explores how and what participants learn as a result of their involvement in collective action, how social movements educate participants and the larger public, and how they generate knowledge. The second category focuses on the influence of social movements such as feminism or the civil rights movement on formal education. Such influence might be through direct action aimed at advancing legislation or policies or through the introduction of new ideas in educational institutions. Also relevant are the relationships between social movements formal education, and the state – relationships that might involve confrontation or take the form of a partnership. Social movements engage in collective protest and contention when opposing policies affecting educational equity, teachers' working conditions or, more broadly, threats to public education. Partnership and collaboration between the state and social movements might take the form of the state embracing or tolerating movement-sponsored initiatives or, in some cases, formalized partnerships between government agencies and movements.[8]

Social movements aimed at and sustained through the fundamental transformation of teaching and learning across thousands of schools are only recently being documented (Farrell, Manion, & Rincon-Gallardo, 2017; Niesz & Krishnamurthy, 2013, 2014; Rincón-Gallardo, 2016). The knowledge emerging from these movements has influenced in important ways the ideas I present here. The conceptual pieces I have presented so far come together to reframe the problem of transforming pedagogy at scale as one that involves changing culture in a widespread manner.

Large-Scale Pedagogical Transformation as Widespread Cultural Change

The rather minimal impact of education reform on the pedagogical core over more than a century would suggest that radically transforming the pedagogical core in a large number of schools is at best difficult, and perhaps impossible. Sometimes, however, rapid and widespread cultural change occurs. Some examples can be found, among others, in the civil rights movement and its influence in shaking up in important ways the relationships between Black and White Americans, or in the feminist movement and the resulting changes in relationships between men and women.[9] An examination of the processes and the conditions under which widespread cultural change occur can provide useful insights on how to radically transform the default culture of schooling across entire educational systems.

The book *Culture Moves: Ideas, Activism, and Changing Values* by Thomas Rochon (1998) represents one of the most comprehensive efforts to date to examine how and under what conditions widespread cultural change occurs. In his examination of some of the most prominent instances of cultural change over 150 years of American history – the civil rights movement, the women's movement, the California immigrant farmer's movement, the gay movement, and the environmental movement, among others – Rochon argues that widespread change occurs when new values, ideas, or practices developed by critical communities are taken on by the larger society by movements that spread them in various social and political arenas.

Agents of Cultural Change: Critical Communities and Movements

Widespread changes in culture, Rochon acknowledges, are responsive to changes in the economic and social environments. But they are not simply a function of them. Agents of change, such as critical communities, are fundamental to the process. A critical community is a relatively small network of people who develop shared understandings of a problem and a stance on how to address it. Critical communities have a prominent role in developing new values, perspectives, and practices. In the educational realm, critical communities are groups of people who develop countercultural pedagogical ideas, perspectives, and practices.

The influence of critical communities on widespread cultural change is at best indirect. Their ideas and practices become powerful to the extent that they are adopted by wider political and social movements. While critical communities serve as incubators of new ideas, social and political movements carry these ideas to a wider audience, to provoke critical examination of existing values, and to create both *social* and *political* pressure for change.

The social arena is the world of changing values, identities, concerns, and daily behaviours. Hence its locus is in homes, workplaces, schools, churches, and the larger public sphere. The political arena, on the other hand, is the realm of leaders, movement organizations, and policy demands. While the social arena is where movements help spread familiarity with new ideas and practices, the political arena, they create pressure to achieve institutional or policy change.

The feminist movement, for example, is invested both in effecting legislation concerning women and in changing beliefs and values about the roles of women in society. The civil rights movement is at the same time a political movement that pursued equality between races before the law and a social movement that discredited segregation and promoted a sense of self-worth and pride among Black Americans. Widespread change has to happen at both the micro-level – the everyday activities of movement actors – and the macro-level – the wider structures of political opportunities that enable or constrain cultural change.

In education, the *pedagogical* has to be added the *social* and *political* arenas, to bring specific attention to the dynamics within the pedagogical core, and to the conditions under which people learn to do things differently. Deliberate attention to the pedagogical arena is especially important given the pervasiveness and resilience of the default culture of schooling. Even in the face of deliberate efforts to substantially transform pedagogical practice, the default culture of schooling re-emerges and prevails as teachers and students continue to go about their everyday classroom activities. Focusing on the pedagogical arena is therefore crucial to the prospect of transforming pedagogy at scale. On the one hand, it brings attention to whether and to what extent a new pedagogy is reproducing or transforming the status quo. On the other, it makes us look at how and under what conditions students and educators learn to do things in ways that are fundamentally different from the status quo.

Adding a pedagogical lens to the cases of widespread cultural change examined by Rochon enriches our understanding of the spread of new values in the larger social and political arenas. It directs our attention to the specific everyday interactions between men and women (in the case of the feminist movement), between Black and White Americans (in the case of the civil rights movement), between immigrant farmers and representatives of large food corporations (in the case of the immigrant farmer movement in California). By zooming-in to the everyday interactions between people, we can understand more clearly whether, to what extent, and how, misogyny, racism, unfair treatment of immigrants, and other forms of domination and oppression have been transcended or continue to live in our societies.

To summarize, widespread cultural change in classrooms and school systems occurs when new pedagogical principles and practices developed by a critical community are taken up by movements that spread them in the pedagogical, the social, and the political arenas. The following three chapters will offer principles of action to advance cultural change in the pedagogical arena (Chapter 4), the social arena (Chapter 5), and the political arena (Chapter 6). Below is an overview of the set of nine principles of action that form the body of the book.

Liberating Learning: Principles of Action

The problem of liberating learning at scale is a problem of disseminating countercultural pedagogies to large numbers of classrooms and across entire educational systems. Looked at from this perspective, liberating learning is about catalysing and sustaining countercultural work in the pedagogical, the social, and the political arenas. It requires the emergence of critical communities that develop countercultural pedagogies, as well as the adoption and dissemination of such practices by movements in the social and political arenas. In the social arena, it involves the use of classrooms, communities of practice, and professional networks as sites where movement participants engage in countercultural work, build individual and collective efficacy through small successes, and strengthen their collective identity, solidarity, and capacity as creators of counterculture. In the political arena, it involves making strategic choices and developing strategic interactions with educational institutions to access and leverage institutional power.

For each arena, three principles of action are distilled from the following sources:

- an examination of the history and development of successful large-scale pedagogical transformation movements in the Global South;
- emerging knowledge on current attempts to liberate learning in school systems around the world;
- existing knowledge on whole system change; and
- the author's own experience as a promoter of widespread pedagogical change.

The three arenas of widespread pedagogical change, and their corresponding principles of action are presented in Figure 3.1.

In this chapter, I introduced the idea of *educational change as social movement* as a metaphor with a good fighting chance of overturning scientific management as the dominant set of ideas shaping how we think about and pursue educational change. For the remainder of this book, I look more closely at the core principles of action to liberate learning in large numbers of schools and across entire educational systems.

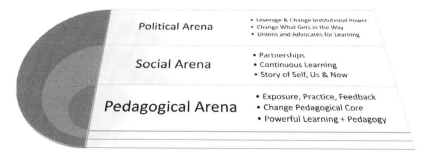

FIGURE 3.1. Principles of Action to Liberate Learning at Scale

Notes

1 Some prominent examples of comparative and international studies on successful educational change include *The Global Fourth Way: The Quest for Educational Excellence*, by Hargreaves and Shirley (2012); *How the World's Most Improved School Systems Keep Getting Better*, by Mourshed, Chijioke and Barber (2010); *Lessons from PISA for the United States*, by the OECD (2011); and *Surpassing Shanghai: An Agenda for American Education Built on the World's Leading Systems*, by Tucker (2011).

2 See for example *Teaching as the Learning Profession* edited by Darling-Hammond and Sykes (1999); *Professional Capital: Transforming Teaching in Every School*, by Hargreaves and Fullan (2012), and *The Allure of Order: High Hopes, Dashed Expectations, and the Troubled Quest to Remake American Schooling* by Jal Mehta (2013).

3 For some of the most recent work and ideas on the promise of professional collaboration and education networks, see *Bringing the Profession Back In* by Fullan and Hargreaves (2016), "Essential Features of Effective Networks in Education" by Rincón-Gallardo and Fullan (2016), and *Collaborative Professionalism: When Teaching Together Means Learning for All*, by Hargreaves and O'Connor (2018).

4 See for example Ken Robinson and Lou Aronica's notion of education systems as agricultural systems (Robinson & Aronica, 2015) and Andy Hargreaves and Dan Fink's environmental view of leadership (Hargreaves & Fink, 2006).

5 This documentary film, released in 2015, examines the history of compulsory schooling in the United States, revealing some of its most important shortcomings in today's world and featuring compelling examples of new approaches to transform learning. The film can be obtained through the following website: www.mltsfilm.org

6 Good accounts on the role of schooling in reproducing dominant patterns of social interaction can be found in the work of Basil Bernstein (1977), Pierre Bourdieu (1974), and Paul Willis (1977). Some good examples of how culture can serve as a playing field to challenge and transform existing patterns of social interaction can be found in the work of Henry Giroux (1983), Anne Norton (2004), and James C. Scott (1990).

7 In their literature review on social movements and education, Tricia Niesz and her colleagues (Niesz, Korora, Burke Walkuski, & Foot, 2018) point out that research on this topic is currently amorphous and relatively scattered. They call for a more unified field with its own identity, rooted on the common ground shared among these studies, which includes questions on pedagogy (whether and how the broader ideas and values advanced by social movements translate into the learning interactions between movement participants), an embracement of critical theory and critical pedagogy (represented most prominently by the ideas of Antonio Gramsci and Paulo Freire), and the notion of research as praxis (with many scholars of social movements being personally involved with and committed to the social movements they examine). The authors suggest that such a unified field, devoted to understanding the educational dimensions and implications of social movements could pose and answer new and important questions related to education. It would also raise the profile of this scholarship and enhance its influence on educational policy, practice, and social movements themselves. While unifying the whole field of social movements and education is beyond the scope of this book, I believe the ideas presented here represent an important contribution to this endeavour.

8 Existing research demonstrates that the relationship between movements and the states is not always one of opposition and contention. It also points out that the movement agenda is prone to being co-opted or incorporated into the existing institutional logic of the government bureaucracy (See for example Gaskell, 2004, 2008; Kane, 2000).

9 My use of the civil rights movement and the women's movement as examples of widespread cultural change is not meant to assume that the visions advanced by these movements have been fully realized. As the recent uprising of white supremacy and the constant upsurge of sexual harassment cases in many spheres of public life in the United States make clear, racism and misogyny continue to be alive and well in contemporary America.

4

OCCUPY THE PEDAGOGICAL ARENA

Transforming the pedagogical core – the relationship between educator and learner in the presence of knowledge – is the most direct way to substantially improve student learning. It is also a powerful way to nurture democracy. The dynamics within the pedagogical core can either reinforce dominant relationships of authority and control suited to authoritarian regimes or build more horizontal relationships of dialogue, mutual learning, and solidarity required for robust democracies.

While it may sound simple, fundamentally transforming the pedagogical core and doing so across large numbers of classrooms and schools has proven to be one of the most elusive challenges for the education sector. As mentioned earlier, even in times when new ideas have sought to fundamentally re-imagine teaching and learning in schools and school systems, the pedagogical core has changed very little, noticeable changes take hold only in a small number of places, and where they do, they don't tend to last long.

It's been over a century since compulsory schooling appeared in the human landscape, and yet many features of schooling remain remarkably stable. These include:

- a clear vertical separation between those deemed to know and those expected to do what they're told;
- a high concentration of authority and control over what, when, and how to "learn" in the hands of those deemed to know;
- the grouping of young people by age;
- an emphasis on covering large amounts of content at the same time and pace for the whole group.

While effective for management and control purposes, these arrangements are ineffective – and even counter-productive – to the purposes of liberating learning.

In Chapter 1 I suggested three reasons why most previous attempts to change the pedagogical core at scale have failed. I will look at these reasons in some detail now. The first common mistake made by education reformers is underestimating the power of the default culture of schooling to neutralize any attempts to transform it. As the popular saying goes: Culture eats strategy for breakfast. Culture is inherently a conservative force that gives its members a sense of familiarity, continuity, and predictability (Evans, 1996). Looked at from this perspective, it should come as no surprise that, no matter how compelling the necessity for change, people in organizations will, for the most part, be reluctant – if not flat out resistant – to abandon the stability and predictability offered by the existing organizational culture. Most education reform efforts either altogether overlook the conservative power of culture in classrooms, schools, and school systems, or simply advance changes that can be easily incorporated into the existing culture, leaving the status quo unabated. A first order of business is to deliberately change the culture of classrooms, schools, and school systems, while constantly reminding ourselves that the default culture will seize any opportunity to strike back and re-establish itself as the default modus operandi.

A second reason for the failure to fundamentally transform the pedagogical core lies in the design of education reforms themselves. Most reform efforts have sought to change the pedagogical core – if at all – *from the outside in*. Some of the common approaches to education reform include things such as changing the curriculum, introducing teacher and principal evaluation schemes, purchasing and delivering the latest technological devices and programmes to schools, creating evaluation systems to assess student outcomes in schools and across educational systems, developing external incentives to reward or punish teachers and schools based on their performance, and so on. These efforts often underspecify how exactly these changes will result in substantively improved teaching and learning. In other words, the *theories of action*[1] underlying most education reform efforts remain vague and unspecific when it comes to articulating the causal mechanisms that will lead from, say, changing a national curriculum, to significantly better, or fundamentally different, teaching and learning.

There is a popular cartoon by Sydney Harris (see Figure 4.1) of two mathematicians standing in front of a blackboard trying to demonstrate a theorem. On the left side of the blackboard is a series of equations representing what they already know. On the right is the result that they seek to demonstrate. In the middle is the following legend: "then, a miracle occurs". Pointing to this middle part, one of the mathematicians tells the other: "I think you should be more explicit here in step two." Most education reforms operate under a "then a miracle occurs" mentality. A more reasonable approach to substantively changing pedagogical practice at scale requires the development of working theories of action that articulate, with increasing specificity and precision, what actions will be tried out and how exactly they are expected to *cause* better teaching and learning in classrooms.

"I THINK YOU SHOULD BE MORE EXPLICIT HERE IN STEP TWO."

FIGURE 4.1 "I think you should be more explicit here in step two"
Source: Copyright © Sidney Harris. ScienceCartoonsPlus.com

Consistent with this perspective, pedagogy is more likely to be substantially trans-formed in large numbers of schools if this is done *from the inside out* (Elmore, 2004). That is, start by articulating as clearly and specifically as possible what you expect students to learn and be able to do; define what pedagogical practices are most likely to cause that type of learning; and identify the conditions at the classroom, school, and system level that will enable adults in the school to learn those practices and to adopt them in their everyday work. Second, work constantly to identify and change the organizational structures, processes, and norms that get in the way of good pedagogy. And, third, sti-mulate continuous interaction between leaders in the central office (be it a school dis-trict, a province, a state, or a national ministry of education) and schools, whereby both parts work and learn alongside each other about what works and what doesn't, refining their work over time based on the observed results. Indeed, this is something that many high performing school districts, provinces, and nations with a sustained trajectory of improvement in student learning outcomes are already doing.[2]

A third reason for the failure to substantively transform pedagogy at scale, closely connected with the previous two, is a deeply entrenched tendency to treat the pro-blem of improving teaching and learning as a merely technical matter. But fundamentally transforming pedagogy at scale is, at its core, a cultural and political project, more so than a technical problem. Social movements, rather than large bureaucracies, have been the most important collective agents of cultural renewal and transformation – especially when it comes to pursuing of causes closely linked to the pursuit of humanistic principles of equality, solidarity, social justice, and democ-racy. In their logic of operation lies the key to radically changing pedagogy at scale.

For the rest of this chapter, I will present and discuss three principles of action to foster cultural change in the first of three arenas that need to be occupied in order to fundamentally transform schooling and school systems: the pedagogical arena.

Craft a Simple and Actionable Vision of Powerful Learning and Pedagogy

Establishing a clear purpose directly linked to student learning and articulating a working definition of the pedagogy(ies) that nurture such purpose is a crucial aspect of changing the pedagogical core. Most districts, provinces, states, and nations articulate in their strategic plans and curriculums their aspirations about what students should know and be able to do as a result of attending school. In many cases, however, these high aspirations are either mere statements of good intentions or tedious and long lists hardly visible in the everyday lives of young people and adults in classrooms and schools. A simple and compelling statement – for example, preparing young people as competent life-long learners, caring citizens, and world changers – is more likely to make its way into the minds and hearts of large numbers of actors across entire educational systems.

Also crucial to the prospects of transforming pedagogy at scale is articulating a simple definition of powerful learning – what does it look and feel like, what are the conditions that enable it? And a clear definition of effective pedagogy – what practices are most effective at liberating learning? What do these practices look and feel like, and how can adults best learn and get better at them?

As discussed in Chapter 3, large-scale pedagogical change occurs when a counter-cultural practice developed by a critical community is taken up by movements that spread it across the pedagogical, the social, and the political arenas. Critical communities may have existed and developed their countercultural practices in the past; they may be contemporaries to people invested in advancing widespread pedagogical change; or they may be formed in the present by agents of change. A wide range of

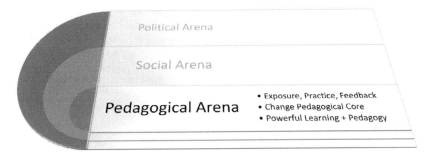

FIGURE 4.2 Principles of Action to Occupy the Pedagogical Arena

pedagogies for liberating learning have been developed for at least as long as compulsory schooling has existed. Some of the critical communities that have developed such pedagogies include proponents of constructivist theories of learning,[3] advocates of critical pedagogy,[4] and de-schoolers.[5] There are living examples of powerful pedagogies around the world, which can be found in school networks such as High Tech High, Big Picture Learning, Envision Education, EdVisions Schools, and Project Lead the Way (Hoffman, 2015; Lathram, Lenz, & Ark, 2016). A global partnership called New Pedagogies for Deep Learning is supporting the development of new pedagogies on the ground in clusters of schools across seven countries, reaching over 1,000 schools in North America, South America, Europe, and Oceania (Fullan, Quinn, & McEachen, 2017). In the Global South, Tutorial Networks or *Redes de Tutoría* (also referred to as the Learning Community Project) in Mexico, Escuela Nueva in Colombia, and the Activity Based Learning pedagogical model in Tamil Nadu in India have managed to fundamentally transform multi-grade schools into learning communities that feature student-centred pedagogies, peer tutoring, collaboration, and democratic practices in thousands of schools.

The definitions of powerful learning and effective pedagogies embodied in initiatives and school networks such as the ones just listed above may vary depending on the purpose, philosophy, and context of each of the critical communities that have inspired their vision and core practices. However, a few core features in common can be identified:

1 Relevance from the point of view of the learner. We can only learn deeply what we're interested in learning. Anything else will simply be superficial and mostly inconsequential. Powerful learning occurs when students (and adults) explore questions or work on projects that matter to them – not because they will get credit, a good grade, or a positive reaction from their teacher, but because they have an intrinsic desire to learn it. This may involve exploring questions that puzzle students (e.g. How come we always see the same side of the moon? How does DNA work? Why do Black and Latino youth make up the majority of the prison population in the United States? How did we get to a point where the top 1 per cent of the world is richer than the remaining 99 per cent?); refining practical, intellectual, inter-personal, or intra-personal skills (e.g. getting better at a sport, at capturing the essence of a complex poem, at thinking as a scientist, at working in teams, at persisting through difficulty); or figuring out ways to make the world a better place (understanding and addressing homelessness; exploring local solutions to tackle climate change; changing the way people relate to autism). Note that I've explicitly stated that relevance has to be seen as such by the student. Telling students that they need to learn something because it's in the curriculum or because they will need it in the future is not very convincing. Where powerful learning is common practice, the curriculum is seamlessly integrated into the work students carry on. As Will Richardson put it, when students are involved in powerful learning, topics and skills in the curriculum are explored *just in time*, that is, when students identify they need them to better understand the issues that interest them, rather than *just in case* – because they may need them in a distant future. Liberating learning almost inevitably involves some menial or repetitive tasks, or memorizing some information, but students do this readily when they know they need it to figure out answers or solutions they are deeply invested in pursuing.

2 Student-led. Young people today seem wired to change the world. The dramatic drops in student engagement and the rise of disruptive behaviour are likely signs of rebellion against a culture of schooling that constrains their freedom, discourages their creativity and critical thinking, and dumbs down their innate curiosity and capacity to learn. When exposed to authentic opportunities for liberating learning, students often labelled as misbehaved or considered less capable thrive. Liberating learning thrives when students have access to multiple opportunities to drive their learning – for example, by giving them the reins to choose what to learn, how to explore their questions or problems of interest, when and at what pace to proceed, with whom to work, or how to assess the quality and depth of their work.

3 Precision of purpose. Students and adults alike develop shared clarity about what students are expected to know and be able to do as a result of the work they undertake in school. Some call it twenty-first century skills, others refer to them as global competencies (creativity, critical thinking, collaboration, communication, character, and citizenship). It's not just about posting the desired outcomes on the wall or writing them down on the blackboard, but about embedding them deeply in the everyday activities of those involved – for example, by encouraging daily reflection on how and to what extent students enhanced their mastery of the desired skills, by embedding in the inquiry projects undertaken by student activities that develop and strengthen those skills, et cetera.

4 Liberating learning as point of departure and point of arrival. In the best examples of liberating learning in action, learning is the work of everyone from the get go, rather than postponed to a later point in time, when students have mastered "the basics". No matter their starting point, students practise learning *as if* they were expert learners from day one. Initial attempts might be imperfect or superficial, but the work gets refined and deeper over time. In this way, the desired result – deep learning and the skill to continue to learn deeply – is brought to the present practice of students.

5 Transparency of the practice of learning. In classrooms where learning has been unleashed, the practice of learning is visible to everyone, all the time: when the teacher models learning in the classroom; when inquiry and study become the work that happens in the public sphere of the classroom; when students create products that demonstrate not only what they learned, but how they learned it; or when they produce and keep multiple versions or drafts of their work to keep track of their progress in mastering new knowledge or skills.

6 High expectations of all students embodied in the everyday practice of educators. Educators who liberate learning embrace the belief that all students can learn at deep levels, and embed these high expectations in their everyday practice. They may do this in a variety of ways: by setting high standards and pushing students beyond their zones of comfort; by supporting students to break through learning obstacles believed unsurmountable; by keeping track of their own biases around race, gender, special needs, et cetera. Holding high expectations for all students is not simply an act of blind faith. Instead, high expectations for all students function as a working hypothesis that educators constantly test, confirm, and refine by observing the impact of changing their everyday practice on the learning of their students. In fact, many educators engaged in liberating learning have learned to set higher expectations *as a result* of trying out pedagogies that liberate learning. It is often the case that when exposed to authentic opportunities for learning, students previously considered less capable by the teacher demonstrate remarkable wit, talent, or skill. Witnessing these surprising "awakenings" of students often serves to dismantle hard-wired biases held by adults about difference in abilities among students.

7 Depth over breadth. Depth takes precedence over breadth. The conventional frenzy to cover all the topics listed in a curriculum subsides. Instead, students work on a smaller number of good questions or topics over extended periods of time. But they do this in ways that cultivate the learning skills that enable them to learn anything they need to learn in the future. When this happens, the official curriculum takes its proper place as a *medium* to deep learning, instead of an end in itself.

8 Public demonstration of mastery. There are multiple ways in which students demonstrate whether and to what extent they have gained mastery of what and how they've learned. These may include texts, videos, audio recordings, or public presentations. Some may keep dossiers with the multiple drafts of the same work or a collection of the learning products they create over time to document their progress. The digitization of learning products of this kind is starting to become accessible and easy to use, and will likely mark a new era in assessment where very robust qualitative evidence on student learning is easy to collect and manage. The adoption of digital technologies and social media has also opened the possibility of creating products for a much wider audience than a single teacher. Blogs, podcasts, and other forms of social media are starting to be used by students to make their work available to anyone in the world. Creating work for the world to see substantively increases the investment of effort and the quality of the work produced by students.

Defining a clear purpose linked to student learning and articulating what powerful learning and its enabling pedagogies look like should not take too long. It should be expected that these definitions will change and be refined over time, as the new pedagogies are tried out in practice and their results observed. It doesn't make much sense to spend a long time at the front end trying to establish a perfect and complete definition of powerful learning and the pedagogies that nurture it. The notion of *minimum viable product* coined in the start-up world (Ries, 2017) might be helpful here. The idea is to get started with the best possible definition available to the group at a given moment, while acknowledging that this starting definition will be "definitely incomplete, and maybe entirely wrong" (Bryk et al., 2015).

The important thing is to establish internal and continuous processes of collaborative inquiry between and among students, teachers, school leaders, and system administrators whereby the initial definitions are tried out in practice, their results monitored, and the designed practices refined or substituted based on the observed results. Collaborative inquiry and continuous improvement will be discussed in more detail later. For now, it should suffice to say that initial definitions of powerful learning and effective pedagogy might be (and perhaps have to be) imperfect at first. And this is ok as long as there are processes in place to continuously and rapidly try out, test, monitor, and refine such definitions.

Establishing a clear purpose linked to student learning and a simple, actionable definition of the pedagogies that cause it is perhaps the easiest part. The real challenge lies in translating these visions into the everyday work of young people and adults in classrooms, schools, and systems. This involves fundamentally re-organizing how classrooms, schools, and school systems operate. Considering that most educational systems are not designed to liberate learning, and that in many ways their regular operations get in the way, this is a titanic challenge. But it is doable. The paragraphs and chapters that follow will offer some core ideas to do this with a good chance of winning.

Deliberately Change the Pedagogical Core

Continued attempts to transforming the pedagogical core from the outside-in will keep producing the same dire results. As Albert Einstein is credited with saying, insanity is doing the same thing over and over again and expecting to get different results. In the new logic for educational change I'm proposing here, the pedagogical core is transformed *from the inside out*. Said in other words, deliberately transforming pedagogical practice is the *starting point*. There are good reasons why this approach has winning chances.

Directly transforming the pedagogical core untaps powerful energy to transform classrooms, schools, and school systems. It triggers and feeds the intrinsic motivation of students to learn, as well as the intrinsic motivation of adults – inside and outside schools – to enhance the learning and the lives of young people. Like the nucleus of an atom, where tremendous energy resides, huge transformational power lies within the pedagogical core, waiting to be untapped. When the pedagogical core is changed directly, powerful energy is released that can mobilize young people and adults to go deeper, to spread their learning practice beyond their sites, and to organize to change what gets in the way.

There are few things as inspiring for educators, families, and communities than seeing young people in a state of *flow* trying to figure out solutions or make meaning of questions that capture their hearts and minds, or seeing them continue to work on their own after school and on the weekends. Few things are as fulfilling as witnessing palpable growth in their ability and confidence to take control over their own learning, or seeing the sparkle in their eyes when they figure things out. Liberating learning stimulates young people and adults to pursue more and more challenging work. And, perhaps more importantly, it propels them to share what they've learned with others. This is how *liberating learning* works as a force for widespread change. Experiencing powerful learning is a liberating experience. And when it comes accompanied with the uncontainable desire to support the learning of others, learning is unleashed, spreading to other sites and across entire educational systems.

The most vibrant examples of liberating learning suggest that deliberately transforming pedagogical practice unleashes and feeds the intrinsic motivation of young people and adults. In those places and systems where learning has been unleashed, you will find clear signs of enthusiasm and clarity of purpose, all the way from classrooms to districts, states, provinces, or even nations. These examples may be only in the beginning stages of fully liberating learning, but they suggest that directly changing the pedagogical core has powerful effects on the intrinsic motivation of young people and adults.

This is consistent with what Daniel Pink (2009) explains about a new generation of organizations that have found the key to their success in nurturing the intrinsic motivation of their workers, rather than relying on external incentives. Organizations and companies such as Wikipedia and Google have been designed to grant people the four conditions of intrinsic motivation: purpose, mastery, autonomy, and connectedness. The logic of scientific management that has pervaded how most companies and organizations are run is built on the core assumption that work is boring and unfulfilling. From this perspective, the common sense way to get people to do the work is to break it down into repetitive tasks that can be mechanically completed, divide up the work among different groups of people, and establish a system of rewards and punishments to reinforce positive behaviour and discourage negative behaviour. When it comes to liberating learning, the core assumption that work is inherently boring and meaningless is fundamentally wrong. Student-led, purposeful learning is one of the most exciting and intrinsically meaningful activities young people and adults can undertake.

There are two tremendous reservoirs of talent and energy that remain latent and waiting to be untapped to fundamentally change classrooms, schools, and educational systems. The first is to be found in the curiosity and natural disposition of young people to learn, and their drive to change the world. Few things can be as intrinsically motivating as learning something that matters to you and serves a purpose larger than yourself, doing it on your own terms (e.g. deciding what, when, how, and with whom to engage in learning), getting better over time, and doing it in collaboration with others. The question of how to "motivate" students or fostering "student engagement" has been very prominent in the education sector. If we are asking ourselves this question so much, it is perhaps because we have come to resign ourselves to the belief that most of what we're asking students to do in school is not internally motivating, but that they have to do it anyway for their own good.

We have to turn the problem on its head and ask what matters to our young people and, using those interests as the entry point to a longer journey, nurture the knowledge and skills required to become deep learners, critical and creative thinkers, problem solvers, good team members, caring citizens, world changers, and so on. It is time to create multiple opportunities for our young people to constantly get better at the practice of learning and to demonstrate publicly (to their peers and the world) what and how they are learning. It is time to create the conditions for students to practise their individual and collective freedom to decide what to learn, how to learn it, when and for how long, and with whom. And it is time to unleash the desire of our young people to connect with other peers and adults to change the world and get better at their learning. When the four conditions of purpose, mastery, autonomy, and connectedness are granted, the question of student motivation won't even cross our minds.

Historically, students have been seen and treated as the "recipients" of education reform. Needless to say, youth are more often than not overlooked in decision making in schools and school systems, despite being key stakeholders of public education. This way of portraying young people misses – and wastes – the tremendous transformative potential that lies in their agency to change pedagogical practices, school designs, school systems, and the world. In the logic of educational change as social movement, the agency of students will play a fundamental role. In existing and emerging examples of educational change as social movement, students are taking active roles in teaching and learning: they participate in discussing and finding solutions to challenges they face in school and in their larger communities; they lead efforts to better their world; and they even serve as tutors or trainers of teachers and other adults. What we currently know about the potential of student agency is still on its baby steps.[6] How deeply and widely the untapped energy of youth and children can take us once it's unleashed is one of the most exciting things to look for in the coming years.

The second reservoir of talent and energy lies in the intrinsic desire of teachers (about 60 million of them around the world) to have a positive impact on the lives of young people. There is extensive evidence that the main driver of teacher motivation resides in their sense of individual and collective efficacy – that is, their personal and shared beliefs about their capacity to influence the learning and motivation of their students. Intrinsic incentives such as a sense of purpose and self-efficacy more than extrinsic incentives – such as financial rewards attached to gains in student performance – serve as primary sources of motivation for teachers to stay in the field of education and improve their professional practice.

The fundamental changes to teaching and learning advocated here are likely to unleash the intrinsic motivation of teachers, which is triggered when they witness the power of their students to learn, as well as from the growing sense of individual and collective efficacy that results from seeing the positive impact of their work on the lives of the young people they serve.

Of course, we cannot and should not expect that teachers' intrinsic motivation will be the sole force to liberate learning across entire school systems. A fair salary and decent working conditions do matter. The importance of teachers' working conditions for student learning lies in their role in affecting teachers' individual and collective sense of professional efficacy, their job satisfaction, their morale, engagement, and professional knowledge. That is, teachers' working conditions matter because they affect their intrinsic motivation and thus the quality and intentionality of their practice (Bascia & Rottman, 2011; Leithwood, 2006).

I have repeatedly mentioned the need to fundamentally change the pedagogical core. Now, what do I mean by *fundamentally* changing it? At a first level, the changes I'm referring to are those required to ensure that what teachers ask and support students to do *produce* deeper learning and democratic mindsets and behaviours. More specifically, when I talk about *fundamentally* changing the pedagogical core, I refer to shifting the nature of the three sets of relationships that constitute the pedagogical core: the relationship between educator and learner, between educator and knowledge, and between learner and knowledge. In the conventional culture of schooling, these three sets of relationships are vertical and hierarchical in nature. Knowledge stands over teachers and students in the sense that it is the official curriculum that mandates what teachers should teach and what students should learn (and, in the most obnoxious cases, even when and how each topic should be taught and covered). And when it comes to the teacher–student relationship, there is a clear vertical separation between the one who knows and dictates what needs to be done and the one who is expected to follow instructions.

As I argued in Chapter 3, this vertical separation between knowledge and educators, between knowledge and learners, and between teachers and students is a disservice to both learning and democracy. The most effective pedagogies establish more horizontal relationships of dialogue, mutual learning, and co-construction between teachers, students, and knowledge. Educators enter into dialogue with knowledge and constantly ask new questions to go deeper into what they're yet to learn; they support the learning of their students while learning alongside them about the topic at hand, about the young people they interact with, and about the phenomenon and the practice of learning; and students learn to see their access to knowledge as a conversation with one or more authors, engaging in dialogue with them through text and other materials.

This section is titled *Deliberately Change the Pedagogical Core*. The original title was *Directly Change the Pedagogical Core*. However, the term "directly" only pertains to those engaged in the everyday practice of teaching and learning. It is obvious that any prospects of transforming pedagogy at scale require that educators fundamentally redefine and redesign their practice according to their individual and collective visions of powerful learning and the conditions that unleash it. At the same time, fundamentally changing pedagogy across entire educational systems will only be possible if school and system leaders intentionally and strategically support the transformation of the pedagogical core (thus my decision to settle on the word *deliberately* in the title of this section).

There is a growing body of evidence that is making the causal pathway between leadership (in schools and school systems) and improved student learning increasingly clear and precise. The first thing to say is that the actions of school and district leaders can have a positive impact on student learning.[7] The influence of effective school and system leaders on student learning is by necessity indirect, but it is nonetheless deliberate. Let's look at this more closely.

Viviane Robinson and her colleagues (Robinson, Lloyd, and Rowe, 2008) have examined the effects of a diverse range of school leadership practices on student outcomes. Of all these, the single school leadership practice with the highest positive effect on student outcomes is participating as a learner in the professional learning of teachers. This single practice has an effect on student outcomes that is at least twice as large as the effect of any other school leadership practice. Michael Fullan (2014) has coined the term "Lead Learner" to refer to school leaders who indirectly but intentionally improve teacher practice and student learning by creating the conditions for all to learn, *while learning alongside them* about what works and what doesn't.

A similar finding is starting to emerge at the school district level. In their study of five high performing school districts in the United States, Susan Moore Johnson and her colleagues (Johnson et al., 2015) found that what explains these districts' high performance and continuous improvement is not whether they are centralized or decentralized, but their ability to effectively manage the relationship between the central office and schools. This includes: a) Providing supports and building capacity to make good decisions; b) Establishing channels for constant two-way communication and mutual learning; c) Creating opportunities for schools to learn from one another; and d) Organizing the system so that it makes sense in the minds and hearts of all involved.

This same logic of action holds true for system leadership at the provincial and state levels as well. Be it high performing systems like Ontario or Alberta in Canada, or in the case of successful large-scale pedagogical change initiatives in the Global South, such as Escuela Nueva in Colombia and Tutorial Networks in Mexico, system leaders created capacity building units within their respective Ministries of Education, which established channels for continuous two-way communication, support, and mutual learning and development between the Ministry, districts, and schools (this is discussed in more detail in Chapter 6).[8]

In addition to enabling two-way communication and collaboration and acting as *lead learners*, one of the most powerful things school and system leaders can do to deliberately transform the pedagogical core is to create the conditions and incentives for teachers to learn how to change their practice. Any effective theory of action aimed at fundamentally transforming teaching and learning will have to be precise on how and why teachers will want and learn to change their practice. I will discuss this in more detail in the section below and in Chapter 5.

Enable Constant Exposure, Constant Practice, and Constant Feedback

Let's think for a moment about the key conditions that allow us to learn new skills. Let's say you wanted to learn how to dance. The best thing you can do is go to a dance hall where you can see expert dancers in action, as well as other dancers with different levels of skill on the dance floor. You can approach some of them to learn new dancing styles, practise specific moves, refine your overall dancing skills, and so on. You also need to get to the dance floor and dance – however imperfectly at the beginning. While dancing, you have access to multiple sources of feedback as to how well you're doing – the gestures of your dance partner or those around you, whether after a certain move you end up stepping on your partner's foot, et cetera. If you pay attention to and act on these sources of feedback, your dancing skills will improve over time.

Whether it is dancing, playing soccer, doing carpentry, conducting scientific inquiry, or any other complex activity, learning requires constant exposure to the practice in action at different levels of expertise (all the way from novice to expert), multiple opportunities to practise the required skills, and constant feedback to know how well we're doing. Let's look at some of the most compelling evidence to date on the power of constant exposure, constant practice, and constant feedback on the learning of new practices and behaviours.

We'll begin with constant exposure. MIT professor Sandy Pentland (2014) has pioneered social physics, an emerging science that studies patterns of social interaction and their effects on individual and collective behaviour, productivity, and innovation. Social physics is demonstrating that the most powerful forms of learning are social in nature. As it turns out, social interaction has a far more powerful influence on individual behaviour than was once believed. The likelihood that we will adopt a new behaviour – everything from our diet, to exercising, to wearing a helmet while riding a bike, to adopting green technologies – is a direct function of the degree to which people around us exhibit such behaviour. The degree to which a person is exposed to a given behaviour predicts their adoption of the behaviour as accurately as IQ predicts academic performance, and more strongly than any other predictor you can think of (e.g. who you are or the behaviours and beliefs of your friends). Of course, people can decide to move somewhere else if continuously exposed to a behaviour they don't like. But if they stay, they are much more likely than not to adopt it. An obvious corollary is that fundamentally changing pedagogy requires constant exposure to the practice of accomplished educators with demonstrated expertise on the pedagogies that liberate learning.

Constant practice is the second key condition to enable the learning of new skills. In his classic book *Outliers*, Malcolm Gladwell (2008) popularized the 10,000-hour rule, attributed to Anders Ericsson. According to this rule, 10,000 hours of intentional practice is what you need to gain mastery of a specific skill or domain. Be it Bill Gates becoming one of the best computer programmers as a teenager or the Beatles becoming the most legendary music band in the twentieth century, the magic number of 10,000 hours, Gladwell argues, seems to come up over and over again as the approximate number of hours it takes to become a master of your trade. The important thing to note is that this number of hours refer to the time invested in *deliberate practice*, that is, practice that you undertake with the deliberate intention of getting better and acquiring full mastery. Or, said differently, 20 years of teaching experience is not the same as 1 year of teaching repeated 20 times. The 10,000-hour rule suggested by Gladwell has been criticized as too simplistic and inaccurate by some scholars of expert performance.[9] Some have pointed out that the number of hours of deliberate practice required for masterful performance varies widely among people and between domains. Regardless of the accuracy of the figure, however, deliberate practice continues to be regarded as crucial to gain mastery of practically any complex activity.

If educators are to get comfortable with and gain mastery of the pedagogies required to liberate learning, they need access to multiple opportunities to try out and practise new pedagogies. The good news is that teachers spend most of their waking hours in classrooms, which offers lots of time to practise. What's crucial is finding ways to effectively occupy the majority of those hours deliberately practising pedagogies that liberate learning.

The third key condition to enable learning is constant feedback. In order to master any practice, we need sources of information on how well we're doing, what we're yet to learn, and what we need to change, refine, or stop doing. When it comes to activities such as dancing or playing soccer, you get immediate feedback in response to your actions. You can observe the gestures of your dance partner in response to your moves. You can see whether the soccer ball you kick helps your team move closer to scoring a goal, is intercepted by your rival team, or goes out of the field.

In the case of teaching, sources of feedback may be subtler, as a lot of the learning that occurs is rather invisible (it happens in the brains of students and in the interactions between them). There are, however, multiple ways to make the learning of students visible, offering some direct sources of feedback. These include engaging in one-on-one dialogue with students to discover how they're thinking about the topic or problem they're working on, explicitly asking them to articulate – in their own words – what they're doing and why, encouraging them to produce work that displays not only what they're learning but how, and many others.[10]

Another important source of feedback is the people around us. Giving and receiving feedback, however, is very difficult. And this is especially true in the education sector, where opening the professional practice of teachers and leaders to scrutiny can be scary and overwhelming. As Michael Fullan (2015) points out, "people don't like feedback and want to be free from it" (p. 69). The highly controlling environment of schooling, where teachers are expected to know all the answers in the eyes of students, principals are expected to know all the answers in the eyes of teachers, and system leaders are expected to know all the answers in the eyes of all of the above, is not very conducive to constructive feedback. And formal mechanisms intended to serve as feedback, such as student evaluation and teacher and principal appraisal, often have the opposite effect: they shut people off rather than opening them up to learning and growth.

Beyond the inadequacy of the institutional environment of conventional schooling, giving and receiving good feedback is difficult because it occurs in the interplay between three core desires we all share as humans, but that are in conflict with each other: our desire to learn, our desire to be liked, and our desire to like ourselves. As Douglas Stone and Sheila Heen (2014, in Fullan, 2015, p. 71) put it, "Receiving feedback sits at the intersection of [...] our drive to learn and our need for acceptance" (Stone & Heen, 2014, p. 8).

Feedback has been mostly overlooked in the educational change field, a trend that is evident in the relative absence of literature on the topic. However, in its relative simplicity (it comes down to talking with honesty, candour, and care about each other's practice) lies an untapped source of renewal for the education sector.[11] Despite its relative absence in the literature, there are a few core guidelines to give and receive good feedback, and more broadly to create organizational cultures where good feedback is embedded in the everyday lives of students, educators, and administrators. At the personal level, Fullan's (2015, p. 77) advice is to turn feedback into

> something you actively seek. [...] If you have to decide whether to err on the side of being worried about acceptance versus [...] learning, choose learning. Once you get past the initial fear of seeking feedback, you will gain on both the learning and acceptance counts.

At the organizational level, Fullan offers a helpful overarching principle of action, which he summarizes as "candor and respect for autonomy". This means that both the giver and the receiver of feedback establish a shared agreement that the giver can offer direct, candid feedback on a particular matter, while the receiver is free to decide whether or not to take it. As a good complement to this principle, Kim Scott (2017) invites people to give feedback that simultaneously challenges directly and cares personally.

To create organizational cultures where good feedback is encouraged, welcomed, and used by all, Fullan (2015) identifies five core things to develop:

1. An overarching and inspiring sense of purpose.
2. Quality relationships.
3. Good, transparent evidence of impact.
4. Candour of feedback infused with a developmental purpose.
5. Respect for autonomy.

In a culture of this sort, opening one's own practice up to the competent and caring eye of peers, students, and leaders – in the form of joint work to examine student work, visiting each other's classrooms to observe teacher practice in action, and so on – becomes the new normal.

Now, cultivating openness to feedback, both personally and organizationally, is not enough. It is also crucial to learn to give *good* feedback. For this, it is helpful to bring attention to one of seven principles of the instructional core proposed by the Harvard team that has popularized and fostered instructional rounds (City, Elmore, Fiarman, & Teitel, 2009): *Description before analysis, analysis before prediction, prediction before evaluation.* Good feedback requires the development of a common, increasingly precise, language among those invested in liberating learning. This is best achieved by avoiding general interpretations of what we observe – e.g. "students were very *engaged*" – and instead starting off by describing with as much detail and precision as possible the actual tasks that we observe others doing while in the process of learning. Only *after* articulating a precise description of what we observe shall we continue with *analysis* – breaking down our observations into categories that help us explain whether, to what extent, and how deeply, student learning is happening. Next comes *prediction*: What should we expect will be new understandings or skills developed by the learners as a result of the tasks we observed them do? If you were a learner in the setting you just observed and did exactly what you were asked to do by the teacher, what would you learn how to do? And only after description, analysis, and prediction, you may get to evaluation: How deep is the learning taking place? What is the next level of work in the setting you just observed?

Constant exposure, constant practice, and constant feedback are basic conditions to learn new practices or adopt new behaviours. As any complex practice, learning to support students to learn deeply, as opposed to getting them to do what we want them to do, requires constant exposure to the pedagogies that we seek to advance, multiple opportunities to try out and practise the new pedagogies, and constant feedback on how well we're doing and what and how we can do better. These three basic conditions for learning have proven true across teacher collaboration groups that effectively improve teaching and learning. This time around, these conditions will have to be developed in the service of the radical pedagogical transformation required for the future.

The direct experience of liberating learning among teachers and other adults, the observable impact of the new practice on the engagement and learning of their students, and working on a shared project of pedagogical renewal with other colleagues can trigger the desire of many to spread their new practice to other schools. This can be pursued by hosting school visits for teachers, administrators, and researchers, organizing school exchanges, showcasing the new practices and student presentations in public events, et cetera. Having multiple opportunities to work with, observe, and help improve the work of others helps build a sense of collective identity that deepens the commitment of participants to transform their practice and entices others to join this collective endeavour. Liberating learning spreads by "contagion".

Notes

1 The concept of *theory of action* was coined in the organizational learning field by Chris Argyris and Donald Schön (Argyris & Schön, 1978). A theory of action is a statement or a series of interconnected statements that causally link intentional actions with their intended results. A good theory of action has three key features: 1. It is a *statement of causal relationship* – that is, it articulates what specific actions will cause the intended results; 2. It is *empirically falsifiable*, meaning that it can be tested and either confirmed or rejected; and 3. It is *open ended*, that is, it can and should be constantly revised and refined based on the results of testing it in practice. A great adaptation of the concept of *theories of action* to the education field can be found in chapter two of the book *Instructional Rounds* by Liz City, Richard Elmore, Sarah Fiarman, and Lee Teitel (City et al., 2009).

2 Many effective school districts across North America have been featured in case studies that describe how they manage to maintain a strong focus on improving instructional practice and developing effective relationships of collaboration, support, and mutual learning between central offices and schools (See Brandon, Hanna, & Negropontes, 2015; Fullan, Rincón-Gallardo, & Rodway, 2017; Fullan, Rincón-Gallardo, & Watson, 2016; Johnson et al., 2015; Zavadsky, 2009).

3 Some proponents of constructivist pedagogies include John Dewey, Maria Montessori, and Jean Piaget in the early and mid-twentieth century. More recent constructivist educators include Eleanor Duckworth, Howard Gardner, Deborah Meier, and Ted Sizer.

4 Some proponents of critical pedagogy include Jeff Duncan-Andrade, Ernest Morell, bell hooks, Peter McLaren, and Joe Kincheloe.

5 Prominent de-schoolers include Grace Llewellyn and John Taylor Gatto.

6 Youth activism, advocacy, and agency have been the focus of a growing body of work in educational research. Some important publications in this field include Michael Fielding's (2001) *Students as Radical Agents of Change*, Ginwright and James' (2002) *From Assets to Agents of Change*, and Ben Kirshner's (2015) *Youth Activism in an Era of Education Inequality*.

7 Two of the most important publications describing the effects of school leadership on student outcomes are a literature review by Kenneth Leithwood, Karen Seashore-Louis, Steve Anderson, and Kyla Wahlstrom (Leithwood et al., 2004) titled "How Leadership Influences Student Learning", as well as a meta-analysis by Viviane Robinson and colleagues (Robinson et al., 2008), which examines the effect of different school leadership practices on student outcomes. These results are further explained in Viviane Robinson's *Student-Centred Leadership* (Robinson, 2011). With regards to district leadership and improved learning outcomes, three series of case studies stand out: *Achieving Coherence in District Improvement: Managing the Relationship Between the Central Office and Schools* (Johnson et al., 2015); *Bringing School Reform to Scale: Lessons from Award-Winning School Districts* (Zavadsky, 2009); and *Superintendents Who Lead Learning: Lessons from Six Highly Successful School Jurisdictions* (Brandon, Hanna, & Negropontes, 2015).

8 Some good accounts of the strategies used by these education systems and large-scale pedagogical change initiatives can be found in the following publications: Ontario Reform (Canada): Gallagher, Malloy, & Ryerson (2016); Escuela Nueva (Colombia): Colbert & Arboleda (2016); Tutorial Networks (Mexico): Rincón-Gallardo (2016).

9 In their meta-analysis of all available studies on deliberate practice and performance, Brooke N. MacNamara, David Z. Hambrick, and Frederick Oswald (MacNamara et al., 2014) found that the impact of deliberate practice on performance varied by domain. For example, deliberate practice explained 26 per cent of performance in games, whereas the percentages of the variance in performance for music, sports,

education, and the professions in general were 21 per cent, 18 per cent, 4 per cent, and 1 per cent, respectively. This meta-analysis, however, does not identify what other factors may account for variance in performance. For now, it is safe to claim that deliberate practice matters, although its importance may vary depending on the domain.

10 John Hattie has become the go-to author when it comes to strategies to improve and deepen student learning. He became a leading authority on effective teaching after conducting a meta-analysis of over 800 meta-analyses to identify the teaching practices with the strongest effects on student outcomes. His findings are presented in *Visible Learning* (Hattie, 2009).

11 A few good resources about the practice and culture of good feedback are: Fullan (2015) "Feedback". In *Freedom to Change*, chapter 4 (pp. 67–98). San Francisco, CA: Jossey-Bass; Lemov, Woolway, & Yezzi, E. (2012) "Feedback." In *Practice Perfect: 42 Rules for Getting Better at Getting Better* (pp. 107–138). San Francisco, CA: Jossey-Bass; and Stone & Heen (2014) *Thanks for the Feedback*. New York, NY: Viking.

5

OCCUPY THE SOCIAL ARENA

The social arena is the world of changing values, identities, concerns, and social behaviours. Its locus is in homes, workplaces, schools, churches, and the larger public space. Attempting to achieve change in the social arena is as important for social movements as it is to obtain change in the political arena. The women's movement, for example, is not only invested in influencing legislation concerning women's rights but also on changing beliefs and values about the roles of women in society. The civil rights movement not only pushes for new institutional arrangements that level the playing field between Black Americans and their White counterparts, but also seeks to discredit the practice of segregation in the public space and spread a sense of pride and self-worth among Black people. The environmental movement pursues legal changes that encourage preservation and discourage environmental degradation but is also invested in raising ecological awareness and changing consumption and disposal behaviours (Rochon, 1998).

In a similar vein, the most effective social movements for educational change do not limit their focus to pursuing legislation and policy to enhance educational quality and equity, but also to making fundamental shifts in at least three dimensions: how adults and their institutions interact with young people, how education systems interact with educators, and how schools interact with the communities where they operate.

In the social arena, the optimal forms of organization are those that enable robust interaction and participation. Within educational systems, classrooms, communities of practice, professional networks, and networks of schools can serve as venues where new pedagogies are tried out, consolidated, and disseminated to new sites. At the same time, movements to liberate learning can only spread into the social arena through alliances with people and organizations outside of schools, including educational bureaucracies, community organizations, advocacy groups, non-for-profit organizations, and the like. In this section I will discuss three principles of action to occupy the social arena.

Political Arena

Social Arena
- Partnerships
- Continuous Learning
- Story of Self, Us & Now

Pedagogical Arena

FIGURE 5.1. Principles of Action to Occupy the Social Arena

Craft and Spread the Movement's Public Narrative: Story of Self, Us, and Now[1]

Story is a defining feature of social movements. By crafting and spreading their public narrative, movements shape their collective identity, encourage their members to act in the face of remarkable odds, and communicate their cause to the world. While strategy is about *how* to act – mapping out existing resources, analysing how to use them effectively, identifying opportunities, pondering pros and cons of different courses of action – story is about *why* – why we're doing what we're doing, why our actions matter, why we care.

Social movements rely on voluntary participation, and one of their greatest challenges is to encourage large numbers of people to overcome the emotions that maintain the status quo – fear, apathy, inertia, self-doubt, a sense of isolation – and engage in purposeful action. For this reason, social movements need not only engage the minds of their members, but also their hearts. As cultural psychologist Jerome Bruner (1986, in Ganz, 2009, p. 8) points out, we interpret the world in two major ways: analytically and narratively. Through analytic thinking we engage the mind: we identify patterns, create hypotheses, and test empirical claims. Through narrative we engage the heart: we connect affectively with injustice, hope, and the desire to do what's right. Story is how we translate our core values into action. Social movements use their stories to access and mobilize the emotions that enable human agency. Movement stories bring to the surface an experienced dissonance between *the world as it is* and *the world as it should be*; they link members and their cause to their core traditions, their values, and their sense of personal dignity. They communicate a sense of urgency to take action. They instil hope and the courage to act. And they inspire a sense of efficacy (the belief in one's ability to change the world for the better) and belonging among its members.

Through public narrative, social movements connect the shared experiences of injustice lived by its members with the hope, efficacy, and solidarity required to engage in purposeful collective action, take risks, and undertake the sacrifices required to advance their cause. Crafting and spreading their public narrative is an important leadership practice of social movements, and it becomes more powerful the more widely storytelling is shared among its members. The stories that social movements tell ignite and sustain their most precious and powerful resource: people's willingness and capacity to act.

As Marshall Ganz (2010) explains, the public narrative of social movements is the combination of three stories: the story of *self*, the story of *us*, and the story of *now*. The story of self conveys the values that call one into action. The story of us communicates the values shared by existing or potential movement participants. The story of now communicates an urgent challenge to those values and demands action in the present. To illustrate these three forms of story, I will draw on the public narrative articulated and used by leaders and educators in the Learning Community Project (LCP, also known as tutorial networks) in Mexico, a movement of pedagogical change that in the course of a decade (2003 to 2012) spread to thousands of public schools serving historically marginalized communities across the country. The vignette below presents the personal story of Gabriel Cámara (2008), founding leader of LCP.

A STORY OF SELF AND US

"Granted: I am an inmate of a mental hospital." This is the opening sentence Günter Grass uses in his novel *The Tin Drum*. [...] I take this sentence and use it to describe my situation within the educational system in Mexico, where I've been working for many years. As Oscar Matzerath in the novel, I confess I feel like an inmate in a mental hospital: a condition that's undesirable, but somewhat bearable because there's hope to heal.

I grew up in Mexico City [...] in times of religious intolerance. I took the first two years of elementary school clandestinely at home, where my parents were offering refuge to two nuns dedicated to teaching [...] My elementary school certificate, of course, is fake: from a school in Guadalajara I never attended, but where the nuns – I have no idea how – had an officially-recognized elementary school. The informality and loose nature of this edu-cational environment, as well as my own disposition made me lazy. Toward the end of fourth and fifth grade, the nuns, as a deference to my parents, announced that I had passed the grade, under the condition that I went to their home to study during the Summer holidays. I don't remember catch-ing up much, but I always passed to the next grade. And so, I got to the end of elementary school with a spurious certificate. Because the head of the order where the two nuns who taught me was a relative of the Jesuit prin-cipal of a secondary school in [the region of] Tacubaya, I got an automatic pass to middle-school. With these antecedents and my bad habits, middle school turned into an obstacle course. By the end of the first year I had failed one subject: Math. By the end of the second year, I had failed three subjects: Math, English, and Civics. [...] I seemed to be destined to tolerate an educational regime that I didn't want to participate in, ready to skip school throughout the year, to eschew the questions from my teachers, falsify notes of absence, and cheat in the exams – sometimes on my own, sometimes with the help of other peers. As was the case in elementary school, my holidays were fully mortgaged with remedial courses.

But in the Summer break of 1944 my destiny changed. Jorge Elizalde and I lived one home away from each other and we shared everything that is shared during adolescence: games, parties, long chats, and especially the neighbourhood mischiefs. Jorge was a year ahead of me in the same school and had just completed middle-school. With the same tone that we made plans to do anything else, he suggested to teach me geometry. He had just studied it on eighth grade and showed me a book in hardcover titled 'Plane and Solid Geometry,' by Wentworth and Smith. He had especially enjoyed the demonstrations in the book, because it was just a matter of understanding a few axioms and postulates well to demonstrate a theorem, to get to the closing Q.E.D. (*Quod Erat Demonstrandum*, Latin expression meaning "that which was to be demonstrated"), without really having to study much, but rather as solving a puzzle. I became fascinated with learning how to demonstrate theorems of geometry.

I started eighth grade a few weeks later. The math teacher was the same who had failed me before. He was accustomed to randomly calling three students to tell the group, one by one, what we had learned in previous classes. Soon it was my turn to stand by the blackboard. Once I was on the stage, the teacher asked me to demonstrate that the sum of the internal angles of any triangle was 180 degrees. I drew the basic strokes with chalk, while feeling the heavy silence of the group. I started to demonstrate the theorem calmly, without conventional formalities, without any calculations but instead pointing with my finger at different parts of the figure that I needed to make my point. I remember that the silence grew heavier, as if both my peers and the teacher had to recover from what had just happened. The teacher asked me to go back to my seat. As I was stepping down the stage, I heard him tell the group, not to me, what I had never heard or imagined hearing: "this one will be good for geometry."

Some time may have passed before I fully grasped what just happened to me, but what is true is that my school experience changed. [...] I started to study the other subjects with joy, I put extra effort on my school tasks, I talked to teachers, I enjoyed attending class. There was no longer place for the indignity and cynicism with which I pretended to be learning in the past. The most remarkable thing was how easy the past was left behind. The transformation had been instantaneous. The key had been a learning relationship of a different nature.

Jorge Elizalde offered me to learn something that he was enthusiastic about, he encouraged me to take on the challenge, and I accepted it freely. I learned to demonstrate theorems in direct dialogue with Jorge, being aware at every moment of my progress, when I could go on my own, when I gave up and needed help. We invested the time that was necessary until we both felt satisfied. There was no obligation, no schedule. But, at the same time, I had never been invested in studying the way I was now studying geometry.

Looking back, I wonder why it took me so long to have an encounter like the one I had with Jorge. Obviously, there were teachers willing to help me learn before I was in eighth grade; there must have been themes in class that I was interested in. But what had not occurred was the personal encounter of the nature of the one I had with Jorge in the Summer holidays of 1944.

This explains my intention to enable and prioritize these type of encounters over external requirements such as predetermined themes and times, formalities and titles, grades and levels. What the geometry teacher told my class when I was heading back to my seat sealed the transformation that Jorge provoked in me, freely and generously: As an act of friendship. It also sealed my desire to do whatever was in my hands to prevent others from inhabiting the underworld that was school for me for so many years. But more pressing than avoiding the discomfort and shame of schooling is my desire to help people see what they're able to do; provoke their surprise, like I was surprised one day when I discovered that I was able to learn and enjoy learning. That's how I explain the stubbornness with which I have sought in my professional life to enable personal relationships and avoid the absurdity of passing years in schools pretending like you're learning under the vigilance of teachers who don't realize or don't know how to bring academic and moral deterioration to a stop.

(Cámara, 2008, pp. 9–14)

Stories of self help listeners connect personally with the experience of the narrator. In his narrative, Gabriel Cámara confides to doing things as a child that many of us would publicly consider reprehensible – skipping class, cheating. He reveals that his parents were accomplices in the game of schooling – accepting his "passing" to the next grade regardless of little evidence of progress, a fake certificate, getting him into middle school through a personal connection of the family with the principal. By doing this, he opens up the opportunity for readers to look at their own histories of cheating and simulation in school (I bet we all have histories of this kind). Gabriel also presents the daunting presence of his geometry teacher and the intimidating practice of getting kids on stage to respond to a question on the spot, an experience many of us remember clearly – and often not very fondly.

Stories of self also communicate hope. Gabriel's self-portrayal as a child that adults had given up on and who by all forecasts was destined to fail in school heightens the sense that personal transformation is within anyone's reach. The liberating learning experienced by Gabriel happened through dialogue with a friend who mastered what Gabriel wanted to learn, a possibility within reach to anyone. The solution to his disconnect with school is so simple that Gabriel wonders why it took so long to have an experience of this kind. And the transformation he experienced is profound. He notices how easy it was to leave past habits behind after the liberating experience that came from learning through personal dialogue with a friend.

And, finally, stories of self offer an answer to the question of why. Gabriel's determination to dedicate his life to enabling personal learning encounters between someone who knows and someone who wants to learn comes from his two-fold desire of preventing others from enduring the boredom and mean-inglessness of school, and helping them discover the liberating power of learning, just as he did in the Summer of 1944 with Jorge.

The *story of us* articulates the values, beliefs, and experiences shared in common with movement participants. It helps to shape their collective identity. Gabriel Cámara's personal story creates several openings for others to identify with his experienced disenchantment with schooling and his liberating experience of learning. His experienced disconnect between schooling and learning, feeling like an inmate of a mental hospital, is likely shared by many.

In the most vibrant movements, stories of self are not only crafted and shared by formal movement leaders. Storytelling becomes a regular practice for large numbers of movement participants. Connecting with and among each other to share personal stories of struggle and transformation – e.g. experiencing powerful learning, witnessing the power of learning in students, or overcoming a major obstacle to install new pedagogies in a classroom, school, or system – help build a sense of collective identity, instil the belief that change is plausible, and nurture feelings of hope, solidarity, and commitment to act. And this brings us to the story of now.

The *story of now* communicates the need to act. Grounded in the values at play in the stories of self and us, the story of now articulates a call to challenge the world as it currently is and to build a world that is more in tune with core human values held in common among movement actors, such as connection, solidarity, justice, equality, and freedom. As Marshal Ganz (2009) puts it, "in the story of now story and strategy overlap because a key element in hope *is* strategy – a credible vision of how to get from here to there" (p. 18). As an example, the vignette below presents Gabriel Cámara's (2008) proposed solution to the challenge of turning conventional classrooms into vibrant spaces for learning.

A STORY OF NOW

Instead of the massification of a conventional class, we work to ensure that each student discovers within the repertoire of manifest knowledge and skills of tutors in the group what they are interested in learning; that they choose what to study and determine their time and pace; and that each have access to the type of personal attention that an apprentice requires. What we will present here [in the book from which this quote is taken] is the strategy that we arrived at after much trial and error, and which allows us to say, grounded on real results, that it is possible to develop genuinely engaging relationships of shared work between educators and learners [...] *Tutorial relationships* is how we call the personal relationships that have been established in ordinary public schools, between adults and young people, and among students. We call them *tutorial relationships* to specify that at their core is the encounter between someone who wants to acquire a concrete competence and someone who has such competence and invests the necessary effort to ensure the apprentice acquires it. For us, this tutorial relationship is the key to transform the educational system from the ground up, as it produces quality learning and teacher satisfaction.

As progress becomes evident, the spread of the change will come, we trust, from teachers themselves. They are the drivers of change as they spread their enthusiasm to their fellow teachers, their coaches, their supervisors, and all the way up to leaders in the State and national systems. [...] As John Taylor Gatto (2006) says [...] "practically everyone can learn almost anything, as long as we secure a few basic conditions, which are not even hard to secure" (p. 345). The tutorial relationships that lead to the creation of learning communities and feed the interest to learn and teach others, confirms that it is possible to secure these basic conditions, because all those who have experienced it have been able to teach and learn from others. Change is possible because it's already happened.

(Cámara's (2008, pp. 14, 15, & 180)

Through the story of now, movements turn the desirable future into an achievable prospect, into something that is within reach if participants engage in purposeful action. Through their combined stories of self, us, and now, movements can inspire and sustain collective action by mobilizing the intrinsic motivation of participants, constructing new individual and collective identities, and nurturing the courage to act.

Cultivate Robust Interaction and Continuous Learning

The frequency and quality of relationships between people in an organization are important determinants of its organizational health, its impact, and the sustainability of its success.[2] This is especially true for social movements, which rely heavily on voluntary participation and often require that participants take significant risks. Taking action to fundamentally challenge and change the status quo is often inhibited by emotional dispositions such as inertia, apathy, fear, isolation, and self-doubt. Frequent and effective interaction with comrades sharing a common purpose can enable purposeful action by stimulating emotions that overcome inhibition, such as a sense of urgency, anger, hope, solidarity, and efficacy (Ganz, 2010).

Strong relationships among peers and between leaders and members are also crucial to develop capacity to act effectively and in coordination, to nurture a sense of collective identity, and to build shared mindsets about the nature of the work – or what Michael Fullan and Joanne Quinn call *coherence* (Fullan & Quinn, 2015). In this section I will discuss how strong ties within a social movement – both laterally among peers and vertically across different levels of leadership – help develop strategic capacity, collective identity, and coherence.

Marshall Ganz (2009) uses the myth of David and Goliath as a metaphor to recount and examine the California Farm Worker's Movement, whose most prominent public face was Cesar Chavez. He explains that *strategic capacity* is what gives the Davids of the world (in this case, immigrant farmer workers in California) a winning chance against powerful Goliaths (major agricultural emporia). According to Ganz, strategy is *how you turn what you have into what you need to get what you want*. Strategic capacity is the capacity to develop good strategy.

Ganz identifies three core sources of strategic capacity that social movements are better positioned to access and use than are their powerful opponents: intrinsic motivation, salient knowledge, and processes of continuous learning. Social movements have a stronger chance to win when the motivation of their members is stronger than that of their opponent, when they have better access to salient knowledge, and when their members use their spaces of deliberation as venues for continuous learning.

Strategic capacity in educational change is to be developed with the two-fold intention of liberating learning and identifying and changing what gets in the way (this latter point will be discussed in more detail in the next chapter). When intrinsic motivation, access to salient knowledge, and continuous learning are put in the service of this two-fold intent, even seemingly small groups of committed people can spur widespread change.

Let's start with motivation, the first ingredient of strategic capacity. Few things are as motivating to educators, administrators, and parents as seeing young people fully absorbed in figuring out solutions or making sense of questions that capture their hearts and minds, gaining confidence in their ability to learn, developing mastery of the practice of learning, and taking on leadership roles. When shared across large enough numbers of people, the intrinsic motivation of adult educators to make a palpable difference in the lives and learning of young people can become stronger and more powerful than institutional motivations to preserve the status quo.

Intrinsic motivation enhances creativity – a fundamental aspect of devising winning strategies. When intensely interested in solving a wicked problem, or when deeply dissatisfied with the status quo, our critical thinking, our concentration, persistence, enthusiasm, and readiness to take risks – in a nutshell, our openness to learning – are heightened (DiMaggio, 1997; Csikszentmihalyi, 1990). And even small wins – for example, when we are successful at deepening student learning or when we get to change what gets in the way – our motivation increases, further enhancing our creativity (Deci & Ryan, 1980). Small wins also help strengthen the collective efficacy of the group[3] – that is, their shared belief that they can have a positive impact on the learning of every one of their students. This in turn enhances their collective identity, or the shared understanding of who they are and what brings them together.

The other two sources of strategic capacity – access to salient knowledge and continuous learning in action – can be cultivated through continuous interaction and collaboration among movement actors. Tony Bryk and his colleagues (Bryk et al., 2015) have developed a promising approach to educational change that uses improvement science to tackle complex educational problems. One of their core principles of action involves developing a deep understanding of the problem, understanding the system that produces the problem, and developing, testing, and continuously refining a theory of improvement to tackle it. These principles of action can be used to liberate learning.

Enhancing and deepening student learning is best pursued through collaborative inquiry, whereby educators engage in joint work to continuously examine evidence of student learning to assess and change their pedagogical practice. Teacher collaboration has been identified as one of the most powerful vehicles for improving student achievement and establishing cultures of continuous improvement.[4] Seen from a social movement optic, the importance of teacher collaboration lies also in the role it plays in building a sense of collective identity around a common cause: liberating learning.

What we know about effective teacher collaboration applies to misleading purposes as well as to worthwhile goals. Teams can get very good at merely raising scores in standardized tests to the detriment of powerful learning. When it comes to liberating learning, it is very important that those engaged in collaborative inquiry constantly come back to the question of what the core results being pursued are and why, as well as whether such results are consistent with what they aspire their students to become.

The second purpose of strategic capacity is identifying and figuring out ways to change what gets in the way of liberating learning. This will be discussed at length in the next chapter. For now, I will say that this is where most of what we currently know about teacher collaboration falls short. Teacher collaboration (in the best scenario) has been so focused on improving student outcomes, that little attention has been given to how the conventional structure and culture of schooling constrain, or even disable, liberating learning. It would seem like, at its best, the idea of teacher collaboration has been restrained to the exclusive purpose of changing classroom practice, while keeping the institutional structure of schools and school systems undisturbed. No doubt the future of education requires relentless attention to changing pedagogy. But to be fully realized, the entire systems surrounding classroom practice (e.g. schedules, assessments, curriculum) have to be fundamentally changed as well, so that they support and enable, rather than constrain and disable, the pedagogies required to liberate learning. This work is not simply to be left to the good will of system administrators. It has to be purposefully pursued by the people who experience the system constraints in their everyday lives – students, educators, and school leaders.

Strategy, as said before, is how we turn what we have into what we need to get what we want. The resources available to educators and leaders invested in liberating learning will vary from school to school and between one educational system and another. In general terms, the resources for strategic capacity available to social movements can be classified as biographical and organizational (Ganz, 2009). Biographical resources include the *identities* of movement participants – that is "the way each person has learned to reflect on the past, attend to the present, and anticipate the future [...] his or her 'story'" (p. 14); their *social networks* – the people and organizations that each member has ties to and can tap into to inform or carry on the movement strategy; and their *tactical repertoires* – the ways members in the group know how to get things done.

Organizational resources include the group's deliberative processes, their resource flows, and their accountability mechanisms. *Deliberative processes* are those communication and decision-making strategies used by the group to develop a shared understanding of the problem they are facing, to activate what they know to craft plans of action, and to reach agreements on the courses of action most likely to lead them to victory. *Resource flows* refer to those tangible and intangible resources that movement actors can use or leverage to mobilize for change. *Accountability mechanisms* are the ways in which shared responsibility and commitment to the group and its cause are developed and sustained over time.

It may seem like the ideas presented in this section refer only to lateral relationships among peers. But these same ideas apply to the development of vertical coordination and relationships across the organizations that social movements seek to influence. Before concluding this section, I will turn to the development of strong collaboration vertically, across multiple levels of an organization.

When it comes to interacting constantly to liberate learning, the work is not only the responsibility of those directly involved in teaching and learning – teachers, students, and school leaders. Indeed, leadership for liberating learning has to be intentionally cultivated across the entire system. Movements for widespread pedagogical change are more likely to succeed when they attract allies and supporters from all levels of the system. Several districts across North America have started to figure this out in their own work for whole system improvement. While very diverse in terms of their size, the students they serve, and the stage in their improvement journey, the strategies for system-wide pedagogical improvement of these districts share six features in common.[5] These shared features, listed and briefly described below, are relevant to developing change leadership at all levels of the organization.

Flat leadership structures. In these districts, every school has a direct link to a senior district leader. This fosters two-way communication between the central office and schools, and makes access to salient knowledge more easily and readily available to everyone across the system.

Widespread teacher leadership. A large proportion of teachers – as many as two in every five – have a formal role as a system leader, which combines supporting the growth and development of their colleagues and providing input, feedback and advice in the development of district-wide strategies.

Constant lateral and vertical interaction. Constant interaction is enabled not only vertically across the organization, but also laterally between schools, through school visits, exchanges, focused professional learning sessions, and the like.

Collaborative cycles of action and reflection across the organization. Leaders across the organization, regardless of their formal hierarchical position, model and practice collaborative inquiry. They examine the impact of their work on student learning, identify the specific practices that explain the results, devise strategies to modify or refine such strategies to enhance their impact, test them in practice, assess impact, and so on.

Changing what gets in the way. Districts are intentional about dealing with distractors, as well as identifying and changing those institutional requirements and practices that get in the way of the pedagogies they seek to spread across the system.

Embracing and encouraging innovation. Senior leaders in these districts deliberately create environments of innovation and risk-taking, where everyone is expected and supported to do things differently, fail, learn, and get better as a result.

Developing leadership across the entire system is crucial for the survival and sustainability of any social movement aimed at liberating learning. Distributed leadership enhances the strategic capacity of movement actors and nurtures its three key ingredients: motivation, access to salient knowledge, and learning practices. By forming strong interpersonal relationships and engaging in constant interaction with other members, leaders can help weave the social fabric upon which the motivation of the group can be sustained. Through ongoing, deliberate interaction to figure out what's going on, what is working and what isn't, they gain constant access to salient knowledge and maintain the flow of learning processes that help refine and modify their strategy over time.

Establish Partnerships to Deepen Learning and Dismantle Systemic Injustice

Liberating learning requires simultaneously changing what happens inside schools and what happens outside schools. These two goals are often treated as dichotomous options in a zero-sum game, where investing in one is thought to lead to divestment in the other. The well-established finding that the socio-economic status of students is the strongest predictor of student outcomes has led some to prioritize the out-of-school conditions that affect the lives of students, such as intergenerational poverty, housing, health, employment, et cetera. On the other hand, the existence of schools that beat the odds – that is, schools serving large proportions of students in historically marginalized groups that obtain much higher levels of achievement than would be expected – has prompted others to focus on changing what happens inside schools to enhance student learning. Advocates of this view also warn about the risk of using the challenging circumstances students face outside of school as an excuse for failure.

Both positions are right. And there is no reason why the problem of changing schools and changing context has to stay framed as a dichotomy. It is possible to establish partnerships that simultaneously enhance student learning and address systemic injustice. At a first level, networks can be created to link schools, communities, and social agencies, where each partner assumes direct responsibility for the portion of the problem most under their control.[6]

But beyond the provision of services to lessen the effects of out-of-school factors on student learning, communities and cities can play a more active role in pushing for educational change and in educating children and youth. The emergence of "education cities"[7] where the infrastructure and institutions of cities (e.g. school libraries, government offices, public parks, museums, et cetera) are put in the service of student learning represents an important development in this direction. Partnerships with businesses and other industries can be established to give young people access to work and professional environments where they learn by engaging directly in real-life work.[8]

Another less explored yet potentially powerful approach to simultaneously changing schools and out-of-school conditions is creating opportunities for students to identify challenges that affect their everyday lives, examine their key causes, and design, test, and continuously refine solutions.[9] Examples of this sort remain small in number and, in general, are bound to individual classrooms and schools. Yet there are a couple of trends that may accelerate the emergence of schools and entire systems that deliberately engage students in understanding and changing their reality. One is the growing sense of urgency to prepare the younger generations to cope with and solve the massive challenges of a volatile and unstable world. Another is the explosion of digital technologies that make access to information and communication across borders readily available.

Relevant here is a new positioning of educational equity, both conceptually and in practice. In the dominant narrative, equity is equated to notions of condescendence, clientelism, and the provision of remedial services. In this narrative, equity is seen as a charitable gesture of the privileged towards those historically marginalized. It is a patronizing stance. Consistent with the new paradigm advanced here – educational change as social movement – the concept of equity acquires a new meaning, consistent with principles of solidarity, compassion – empathizing with, rather than feeling for – and the acceptance of everyone's inherent value as human beings, regardless of race, socio-economic status, gender, sexual preference, nationality, citizenship, or immigration status. Equity is not something to be handed down, but something to be pursued alongside those historically marginalized in the pursuit of the full expression of our shared humanity.

Positive discrimination – giving more to those in conditions of disadvantage to offer a levelled playing field vis-à-vis their more privileged counterparts – is a foundational principle of equity in contemporary societies, a principle that has been accepted in the constitutions of most countries today (See Sarmiento & Colbert, 2018). Recent international evidence supports the claim that educational excellence and equity are not mutually exclusive. Indeed, excellence can and should be achieved *through* equity. As reported by the Organisation for Economic Cooperation and Development (OECD, 2013), in 20 of the 23 top performers in the Programme for International Student Assessment (PISA), the strength of the relationship between socio-economic status and student achievement is below the average of all OECD countries. That is, most top performing educational systems in the world are also more equitable in the distribution of educational opportunities among their young people. These systems are developing excellence *through* equity by removing systemic barriers to access to educational opportunities and investing disproportionately more support and resources to schools serving high proportions of students in historically marginalized groups and communities.[10]

In the repositioning of equity proposed here, positive discrimination is reinterpreted so that it is not only about giving the least privileged *more*, but also, and more importantly, *better*. That is, true equity in schools and school systems is not only about more resources for those historically marginalized, but also about granting them access to the best possible learning experiences through powerful pedagogies and high expectations.

Some of the most powerful movements to liberate learning turn what has come to be framed as "disadvantage" (e.g. high degrees of poverty or marginalization) into opportunities to depart radically from conventional schooling and reinvent education.[11] The sense of urgency that exists in many schools and school systems to improve student outcomes among children and youth most often disengaged in conventional classrooms might make administrators more open to innovation and radical departures from conventional practice. This opens up opportunities to engage traditionally disenfranchised students in exploring questions that matter to them and offering higher degrees of autonomy on what, when, how, and with whom to learn. In conditions of greater freedom and autonomy over their learning, traditionally troublemakers become eager learners and learning leaders.[12] And, as a handful of widespread pedagogical change initiatives in the Global South show (See Chapter 2), children and youth from historically disenfranchised communities who gain access to powerful pedagogies can outperform their more privileged counterparts in just a few years.[13]

In this chapter, I have offered three principles of action to advance pedagogical transformation in the social arena: shaping and spreading the movement's public narrative, cultivating robust interaction and continuous learning, and establishing partnerships to deepen learning and dismantle systemic injustice. One more arena to go: the political arena. This is the focus of the next chapter.

Notes

1 This section draws heavily on Marshall Ganz's work. Ganz (2009, 2010) is one of the most authoritative voices in the social movement and community organizing work in North America. Unlike many social movement scholars, who study social movements from afar, the power of Ganz's work and insights comes from his direct involvement in important social movements in the United States. In his college years, he participated in the civil rights movement, becoming involved in the Mississippi Summer Project and then working for the Student Non-Violent Coordinating Committee. In the mid-1960s, he joined Cesar Chavez and the California Farm Worker Movement, where he served in a wide range of positions for 16 years. He is credited for designing the community organizing model that led to the election of Barack Obama as the first African American president of the United States in 2008.

2 Social physics (Pentland, 2014) is making important discoveries on the causal relationship between patterns of social interaction and changes in human behaviour, productivity, and creativity. Social physics has dramatically enhanced the speed and reliability with which social network dynamics can be described, analysed, and causally linked to relevant outcomes. This new science explores the properties and patterns of interactions between people through a method called *reality mining*, which consists of collecting and analysing rich data on human behaviour captured through personal digital devices. There are three fundamental advantages to this data collection methodology over the methods currently available to social network analysis in education and the social sciences in general. First, it captures real-time interactions between people over extended periods of time, whereas social network analysis so far has relied heavily on individual recall and self-reports of their past interactions. Second, it requires minimal effort from participants and researchers, whereas conventional protocols and processes to capture social network data are taxing and time consuming. And, third, it collects multiple variables simultaneously, in contrast with the small number of variables that conventional social network data collection methods allow. Relative to social physics, research on social networks in education, and in the social sciences in general, is in its infancy.

3 Collective efficacy, that is, the shared belief among teachers that together they can make a positive difference for their students – has been identified as one of the strongest predictors of student achievement, with a much larger effect than any measures of individual teacher practice (Donohoo, 2016). The only meta-analysis on the effect of collective teacher efficacy on student achievement to date is a PhD dissertation by Rachel Eells (2011), University of Chicago. Her various meta-analyses conducted yielded weighted average effect sizes ranging from 0.54 (social studies) to 0.63 (reading). Collective teacher efficacy was found to be strongly and positively correlated with student achievement in all subject

areas measured. There were no differences across school levels. Upon transformation of the effect size to make it comparable to the effect-sizes reported by John Hattie (2009) in *Visible Learning*, the effect is $z = 1.49$, a figure comparable to the most powerful effects across Visible Learning variables. Prior to Eells' meta-analysis, a few dozen studies had examined the relationship between collective teacher efficacy and student performance. The most prominent findings of these studies include: a) collaborative teacher efficacy has bigger impact on student achievement than race or SES (Goddard, 1998; Goddard, Hoy, & Woolfolk, 2000); b) Collective teacher efficacy positively predicts student achievement after controlling for other aspects of school context (Cybulski, Hoy, & Sweetland, 2005; Goddard, LoGerfo, & Hoy, 2004); c) Collective teacher efficacy positively and significantly relates to between-school differences in achievement (Goddard, 2001).

4 See for example Earl & Katz (2005); Hargreaves & Fullan (2012); Little (1982); Stoll et al. (2006).

5 In my role as Chief Research Officer in Michael Fullan's international education consulting group, I have visited, interacted with, and learned from a handful of school districts that embody, or embodied over a sustained number of years, these six principles of action for leadership development across the entire organization. These include the Corona Norco Unified School District, Fresno Unified School District, Garden Grove Unified School District, Long Beach Unified School District, Twin Rivers Unified School District, and Whittier Union High School District in California; the Ottawa Catholic District School Board, the Hamilton-Wentworth District School Board, and the Simcoe County District School Board in Ontario. We have also recently connected and worked with some school districts that embody these practices in the province of Alberta, Canada.

6 Jal Mehta (2013) offers some examples of effective partnerships of this nature, such as a joint effort carried on in Boston in the 1990s to address youth violence and homicide, which actively involved law enforcement, local ministers, youth workers, and a variety of social agencies; community schools that operate jointly between schools and other social agencies to provide after-school care, health, dental and mental health services, et cetera. Another example offered by Mehta is the recent Harlem Children's Zone project that provides a range of services for students, which explain in great part its academic success.

7 See Faure et al. (1972); http://education-cities.com/en/about/

8 A good example of partnership between a school system and the productive sector is the Specialist High Skills Majors in Ontario. The programme offers students in Grades 11 and 12 a wide range of opportunities to focus on a career path that matches their skills and interests through direct participation in the industry of their preference while meeting the requirements for high school graduation.

9 A handful of examples of this sort can be found in the work of advocates of critical pedagogy (Duncan-Andrade & Morrell, 2008), in education efforts directly aimed at bettering the world (Prensky, 2016), in the work of some non-governmental organizations (see for example http://maximumcity.ca/) and through emerging initiatives such as the New Pedagogies for Deep Learning (Fullan, Quinn, & McEachen, 2017; see also http://npdl.global).

10 In their book *Excellence through Equity*, Alan Blankstein, Pedro Noguera, and Lorena Kelly (Blankstein et al., 2015) make a similar point in their examination of turnaround schools, districts, and States in the United States.

11 Some of the most prominent examples of widespread pedagogical innovation that turn "disadvantage" into "possibility" are Escuela Nueva in Colombia (Colbert & Arboleda, 2016; Sarmiento & Colbert, 2017); Tutorial Networks in Mexico (Rincón-Gallardo, 2016), and the Activity Based Learning Model in the Indian southern State of Tamil Nadu (Niesz & Krishnamurthy, 2013, 2014). The countercultural pedagogies advanced through these three educational change initiatives from the Global South have reached thousands of schools.

12 Carla Shalaby (2017) has written one of the most beautiful accounts of the brilliance and wit of *Troublemakers* in school in a book of the same title. A highly recommended read that repositions troublemakers as *canaries in the mine* – that is, as highly sensitive and smart beings that, through their behaviour, are sending us warning signals of the toxicity of conventional schooling.

13 By the 1990s, when Escuela Nueva had become the nation-wide pedagogical model for rural communities in Colombia, reaching 20,000 schools, students in rural schools were outperforming their counterparts in urban schools (with the exception of Colombia's mega-cities). In the case of Tutorial Networks in Mexico, four years after their spread to 9,000 schools, students in public middle schools serving students in the communities with the highest degrees of marginalization across the country out-performed their counterparts in more privileged public middle schools – and, in the case of math, achieved at similar levels to students in private middle schools.

6

OCCUPY THE POLITICAL ARENA

The political arena is the realm of leaders, movement organizations, policy demands, and institutional power. While the pedagogical and social arenas are where movement participants advance change in their everyday work and in their relationships with others, the political arena is where they can create pressure to achieve institutional changes that remove constraints or enable widespread cultural change. Countercultural work in the pedagogical and social arenas is often less visible than action in the political arena, yet it is crucial for the viability and sustainability of system-wide pedagogical renewal. It could be argued that work in the pedagogical and social arenas is the most important work movements undertake. After all, it is in the everyday lives of students, educators, administrators, and allies that the new visions for education advanced by movements have to take root and grow.

At the same time, larger social and political structures can enable or constrain the work of cultural renewal advanced by movements. Societies may vary in the availability and opportunities to form critical communities, in the perception of these critical communities in the wider society, and the openness of the political system to groups pursuing new policy demands. The strategic choices made by movements – whether and to what extent to engage in the political arena – and the nature of their interaction with government – ranging from direct confrontation to collaboration – are shaped by the social and political opportunities movements have, or create, to access decision-making structures in government (Rochon, 1998).

Movements are often conceptualized as opponents to the state, as counter-communities with alternative authority and legitimacy structures (Alberoni, 1984). Consistent with and reinforcing this view, political action in education and the research that documents it have paid a lot of attention to the processes of protest and contention advanced by social movements to oppose policies perceived to debilitate public education, compromise educational quality or equity, or threaten teachers' working conditions.[1]

Useful as this way to think about and study social movements is to highlight the critique of social and political systems advanced by movements, too much emphasis on contentious politics may lose sight of the dynamic interaction that takes place between movements and governments. Movements and states each control resources the other needs. Movements can benefit from leveraging the power and infrastructure of the state, whereas political leaders might benefit from incorporating the energies set in motion by movements for their own political purposes (Rochon, 1998, p. 201).

When movements are able to gain access to decision-making structures in government their relationship with the state is more likely to be one of collaboration and cooperation. When this access is limited, the relationship is more likely to be one of confrontation and critique. How movements interact with governments depends on the strategic opportunities afforded to or created by them. More generally, it depends on the resources available to movements in the social and the political arenas. In a similar fashion, efforts to liberate learning in educational systems will be shaped by the relationships between movement participants and the education system where they operate, as well as by their access – or lack thereof – to influential decision makers.

There are moments when new political opportunities open up, offering the occasion to influence institutional decisions that benefit the cause advanced by movements. These opportunities may come in many forms. A key ally of the movement becomes a formal leader in an influential position at the Ministry of Education. A new set of policies is approved that helps to advance the movement's cause. A politician comes to power with an explicit intention to make education a core priority in his agenda. After years of sour confrontation, a Ministry of Education and the teachers' union reach a new deal to work together to prepare students for the future. A new report by an international agency or a media scandal targets policies that constrain efforts to liberate learning (e.g. high-stakes accountability, excessive testing, administrative distractors to the everyday work of teachers, et cetera). By making strategic choices to leverage or create political opportunities of this sort, movements can influence their institutional environments, make them more welcoming to the cultural change they're advancing, neutralize opposition, and, ultimately, contribute to creating the educational systems of the future.

In the previous chapter I discussed how the public narrative and constant interaction between movement participants help build a sense of solidarity and collective efficacy – the belief that they can make a positive impact in the world through unified action. Political engagement is another distinctive feature of movements. Political engagement helps develop skills and habits that provide movement participants with a sense of liberation from feelings of hopelessness in the face of great odds. If solidarity makes movement participants *willing* to get involved in collective action, political engagement makes them *able* to do it. Through their engagement in movements, participants increase their ability to understand the political and social worlds and to take effective action. The knowledge and organizational skills that movement actors gain through political engagement strengthen the movement's ability to disseminate new values and practices into the culture. Political engagement encourages participants to spread the movement's new cultural values and practices to their families, friends, and other group members, thus widening the circle of those who feel prepared for mobilization while setting the ground for widespread cultural transformation.

The rest of this section offers three principles of action to pursue widespread pedagogical change in the political arena.

Organize to Change What Gets in the Way

As discussed in Chapter 1, schooling was not designed to foster learning or democracy, but rather to provide custody and control, and to distribute merit. These three core functions not only constrain, but even disable, learning and democracy. When teachers and leaders fully embrace the cause of liberating learning, they inevitably experience tension with the existing structures, practices, and norms of conventional schooling. Being countercultural in nature, pedagogies purposefully designed to liberate learning will create friction with the dominant culture and institutional structures of conventional schooling. Seeing them as extraneous objects, the natural reaction of the schooling system will be to expel or devour them.

This is where efforts to change teaching practice to liberate learning often come to a halt. Liberating learning at scale requires negotiation with local and regional educational authorities to modify or lessen the institutional constraints imposed by existing institutional requirements, norms, and procedures. And, more importantly, it requires deliberate organizing to change what gets in the way. This is where strategic capacity can break new ground.

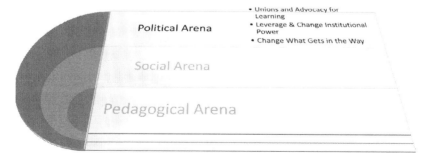

FIGURE 6.1 Principles of Action to Occupy the Political Arena

As said before, strategy is how we turn what we have into what we need to get what we want. The resources – both tangible and intangible – available to educators and leaders who embrace a liberating learning agenda will vary across educational systems. These may sometimes have the form of observable improvement in the learning of their students, rapport with students and parents, or strong experience organizing classroom visits. Sometimes they may have leverage with an influential actor in the field – a system leader, an opinion leader, a renowned faculty of education, or the like. In an instance like this, movement actors could work to identify the institutional structures or requirements that get in the way of liberating learning (say, for example, that the report cards teachers are required to submit are inconsistent with the type of more powerful learning their students are demonstrating), and craft a strategy to bring this tension to the awareness of system leaders with the institutional power to change what is getting in the way.

People in the group could, for example, organize a classroom tour where students invite system leaders, experts, and other teachers to observe what and how they are learning and what impact this learning is having on their lives. The tour could be followed by a forum where students, teachers, parents, administrators, and external experts discuss the impact of the work observed in the classroom, and the extent to which this work is an illustration of what the school system and society want young people to learn and be able to do.

Seeing powerful learning of children and young people in action often makes a deep mark on the minds and hearts of people who witness it, including system administrators. This makes it more likely that they will be open to reduce or change the institutional requirements that get in the way of liberating learning. If agreement can be reached among visitors that what they saw is a living example of the education aspirations of society, then students, teachers, and school leaders could describe the ways in which existing institutional requirements (let's stick to a report card that is inconsistent with the type of more powerful learning going on in the classroom) are constraining their efforts to consolidate and spread pedagogies to liberate learning across new sites. Next would be a deliberative process with system leaders and experts to figure out solutions to the existing tension (e.g. what purpose is the existing institutional requirement trying to fulfil? Is such purpose worthwhile? If so, what could replace the existing requirement so that it helps such purpose while enabling the type of learning observed in the classroom?).

In the previous chapter, I discussed the importance of constant interaction between movement participants to cultivate a sense of collective identity, establish a culture of continuous collaboration to change pedagogy, and develop strategic capacity. In addition to these dense interactions within the group, it is important to connect outwards through the links that individuals within a group have with other people or organizations outside the group. These connections offer access to ideas, knowledge, and expertise that fall beyond the existing repertoire of the group and may offer effective solutions to pressing questions faced by movements.[2] The activation of these external connections may also prove key for movement actors to learn about emerging political opportunities to take advantage of.

Throughout this section I have emphasized ideas to encourage a proactive stance towards transformative work, rather than an openly oppositional stance. There may be instances where new policies or programmes threaten the foundations of powerful learning and democracy. In these instances, and when access of movements to institutional power is limited or non-existent, protest and open political confrontation might be the only reasonable alternative.[3] But protest and open confrontation should be treated as a last resource, rather than the default response. Social movements rely mostly on voluntary participation. Their most precious resource is the time and commitment of movement participants, and this resource has to be used wisely and strategically.

Even in cases when open confrontation is the only reasonable way forward, long-term success will only be achieved if opposition to bad policies – or what Michael Fullan (2015) recently called the "freedom from" stance – is combined with and outweighed by more robust work that is proactive in bringing to life the best possible education we can envision for our younger generations – a "freedom to" stance, in Fullan's terms. Destroying what you hate takes you nowhere if you don't save and nurture what you love.[4] Dedicating most of the precious energy and commitment of movement actors into changing pedagogy in their everyday work and spreading change to other sites and across the educational system is vital to the survival and sustainability of any movement committed to the renewal of public education. On the one hand, this is the most direct way to liberate learning. On the other, it substantially increases the chances of building legitimacy and support from students, administrators, parents, and communities, a support base that can be leveraged if open political confrontation becomes necessary.

Leverage Institutional Power and Change Its Logic

Institutional power can offer tremendous opportunities for movements of pedagogical transformation to spread across entire educational systems. It can offer resources and infrastructure to mobilize change in a common direction, political backing and endorsement of efforts to fundamentally change teaching and learning, or the capacity to develop new policies and tools that help advance the cause of liberating learning.

There is, however, a risk that haunts almost any movement as they interact with institutions: getting sucked into the dominant institutional logic of vertical authority, hierarchical control, and bureaucratization that characterizes most educational systems. The new institutions required for the educational systems of the future – if the future of education is to be bright – have to embody and effectively foster the conditions that liberate learning. In their current format as large bureaucracies with clearly defined hierarchical divisions and a strong focus on ensuring compliance, most existing educational systems are a far cry from the institutions required for the future. Social movements have a crucial role to play beyond organizing to access and leverage institutional power and resources. They should also work to fundamentally change the logic of institutional power.

No matter where the initial drive for pedagogical renewal is coming from in an educational system – the grassroots, the top, or the middle – movement actors should endeavour to shift the nature of their relationship with the other levels. This shift involves moving away from vertical relationships of authority, control, and compliance towards horizontal relationships of dialogue, support, and mutual learning. It involves leaving behind relationships where authority is determined by the hierarchical position one holds in the institution and, instead, nurturing relationships where authority is grounded on genuine legitimacy that stems from the demonstrated commitment and capacity of leaders to spearhead the collective effort to liberate learning in schools and across entire educational systems.

For the rest of this section, I will draw on three cases that I have studied in depth over the past few years to offer some overarching guidelines for action. The cases are: the Ontario Reform Strategy in Canada; the Tutorial Networks in Mexico (also referred to as the Learning Community Project); and Escuela Nueva in Colombia. The key commonality among these three cases is their success at changing pedagogy at scale (5,000 schools in Ontario; 9,000 schools in Mexico; 20,000 schools in Colombia), with demonstrated positive impact on student outcomes. Beyond these commonalities, the cases are widely diverse in terms of the context where they emerged, their locus of development (in one the driving force was at the top, in the other two it was at the grassroots), their theory of action, and their specific strategies. Yet, they share some aspects in common when it comes to leveraging institutional power and changing its logic – the core theme of this section.

Many of the most successful cases of large-scale pedagogical change, diverse as they may be in terms of their context, priorities, strategy, and theories of action, share a handful of political conditions in common that enabled their success. One of the most important is the opening of political opportunities to directly access institutional power. In Ontario, the liberal government that came to power in 2002 after years of labour disruption and public dissatisfaction with education, made education one of its top priorities. In Mexico, a leader of a grassroots pedagogical change initiative that had started to spread to dozens of public middle schools across the country was invited to take a leading position at the Department of Innovation of the Ministry of Education. In Colombia, one of the co-founders of Escuela Nueva was appointed as Deputy Minister of Education. In all these cases, people with expertise in pedagogical change in schools and districts seized the opportunity to access institutional power. At the same time, they worked relentlessly to change its logic.

The creation of relatively independent leadership units with the responsibility to build the capacity of schools and stimulate pedagogical change has proven to be an effective strategy to facilitate change across an education system. In Ontario, this leadership and capacity unit was the Literacy and Numeracy Secretariat (LNS), later called the Student Achievement Office. In Mexico, it was the creation of a central leadership team for a nationwide programme hosted by the Department of Innovation at the Ministry of Education, called at first Program for the Improvement of Educational Achievement (PEMLE) and later on Integral Strategy for the Improvement of Educational Achievement (EIMLE). In Colombia, it was the national team of Escuela Nueva within the Ministry of Education.

As a first step to mobilize the change in culture in their respective systems, each of these units was shaped as a hybrid team that combined practitioners with demonstrated expertise in turning around schools or entire districts as well as people with deep knowledge of and experience within the bureaucracy. The LNS in Ontario attracted leaders of school districts with a record of success for improving literacy in their systems. These district leaders were seconded to work in the Ministry for two years and then sent them back to their districts. The national leader of PEMLE, who had played a key leadership role in the grassroots pedagogical change work of the Learning Community Project, brought into her team many of the teacher coaches who had spent years working alongside teachers to turn their classrooms into learning communities. Vicky Colbert, co-founder of Escuela Nueva, searched for and brought to her national team a handful of talented teachers from rural multi-grade schools who had demonstrated success at turning their schools into vibrant places of learning. The introduction of these units with leading practitioners in their respective Ministries of Education was not without its bumps. With much of their expertise grounded in pedagogy and change at the school and system levels, they were seen as strangers by the most bureaucratically oriented sectors of the Ministry. Yet, these units gained enough political backing to work with relative autonomy to move their strategy forward.

The importance of forging leadership corps of this kind was two-fold. On the one hand, it brought into the Ministries a set of skills and expertise (fostering effective pedagogies and changing the culture of schools) that tends to be scarce in Ministries of Education and yet is crucial to any attempt to change pedagogy in large numbers of schools. On the other hand, it gave the reforms advanced by these teams an initial boost of legitimacy among educators and local administrators. Seen more as "one of us" than as people from the Ministry, these leaders had a better chance to be heard, trusted, and taken seriously by those responsible to carry on change in classrooms, schools, and districts.

But bringing the right people to the leadership team is just a first step. Changing pedagogy at scale also requires establishing working partnerships with educators and local leaders that are grounded in dialogue, co-development, co-learning, and mutual influence. Rather than coming to the field with a solution to be implemented with fidelity, these leadership teams approached schools and districts with some ideas to try out, or with questions to which neither of them had an answer to, but for which they would figure out good solutions together. This is what Michael Fullan (2018) calls *joint determination*. When leaders approached schools with a specific idea or strategy, they kept it open ended, as something to be tried out in practice, its results assessed, and then refined, modified, or all together discarded based on its impact and feasibility.

These leaders also served as brokers who made connections between schools or districts whom they knew could support and learn from each other, helped develop teacher networks, facilitated school visits or district tours, organized learning fairs, and so on. They were intentional about strategically spreading pedagogical transformation. They supported the creation of cultures of collaboration whereby teachers and leaders could come together to examine, refine, and modify their practice. They facilitated the creation of networks to spread the enthusiasm for changing pedagogy between those already on board and those who were more hesitant. They also worked to continuously identify those institutional requirements, practices, and routines that were getting in the way of pedagogical change, developing solutions to either weaken or fully remove such constraints.

These teams worked to create organizational cultures where everyone involved, regardless of their formal role in the institution, was expected to master and publicly practise the core principles of action that were expected from teachers in classrooms and from principals in schools. The LNS in Ontario, for example, engaged in cycles of collaborative inquiry of the same nature as the collaborative inquiry they sought to install in schools and districts. In Mexico's PEMLE, everyone in the programme, all the way from the national leadership to classrooms – teachers and students included – was expected to model and practise the pedagogy of tutorial relationships as part of their regular work. In Escuela Nueva, every participant was expected to know how to use the self-learning guides for teachers and students.

The concept of a *fractal* offers a helpful metaphor to describe the nature of the organizational culture that these leadership units were able to build within their respective ministries of education. A fractal is a geometric shape that remains the same no matter how much you zoom into it or zoom out of it. A simple example of a fractal is a spiral – it remains a spiral no matter how close or far away it is when you are looking at it. In a way, the organizations these leadership teams were able to create were like fractals: you could see the same basic practice at all levels of the system: in classrooms, in schools, in districts, and in the central office.

Another way to describe the configuration of an organizational culture required to advance widespread pedagogical change is as a networked system, rather than a hierarchical bureaucracy. Some of its essential features include flat leadership structures, frequent communication and coordination laterally and vertically, relationships of dialogue and mutual learning, and a tight link between design and execution – whereby designers of a particular change idea take the responsibility to demonstrate its feasibility in practice, continuously refining it based on feedback from the field.

The sustainability of organizational cultures like these in educational bureaucracies remains a massive and elusive challenge. Of the three examples I use in this section, only one – Ontario – survives within its Ministry of Education (and it is yet to be seen what will happen after the Conservative Party won a majority government in the provincial elections of June 2018). In this case, 15 years of political continuity – with the Liberal Party ruling the province since 2002 – were helpful to maintain and grow an organizational culture where the relationship between the central office and school is one based on dialogue, support, mutual learning, and continuous improvement. The Mexican Tutorial Networks and Colombia's Escuela Nueva had a shorter life within their Ministries of Education, although they continue their work through non-governmental organizations. Both initiatives were marginalized or removed from the national agenda when political shifts changed the direction of the Ministries of Education in these countries.[5]

Changing the logic of institutional power is hard work and initial wins will likely be fragile. Political transitions beyond the control of capable and committed educational leaders can wash away years of effort. And, yet, perseverance to pursue a new institutional order in educational systems is of the utmost importance. Only through the creation of new educational institutions where the logic of hierarchical authority, control, and compliance is substituted for a logic of dialogue, mutual learning, and continuous improvement can we expect that our desire to fundamentally transform schools and school systems into places of vibrant learning and robust democracy will be realized.

Link the Work of Advocacy Groups and Unions to the Learning Agenda

It is practically impossible to talk about the political arena in education without thinking about advocacy groups and teacher unions. I will take on the question of advocacy groups only briefly here, and then move on to discuss the work of unions. When talking about advocacy groups I will refer to those groups advancing equity, social justice, and civil rights causes. I am not interested here in organizations supporting charter schools, de-funding public education, and other versions of privatizing public education. Advocacy groups in education have played a fundamental role in placing the spotlight on systemic inequalities and pushing for policies that level the playing field between students from historically marginalized groups (e.g. students of colour, children confronted with intergenerational poverty, LGBTQ children and youth, et cetera) and their more privileged counterparts. This work is very important in any healthy democratic society.

At the same time, the depth of its impact is limited without deliberate attention to the learning agenda. Most of the work advanced by advocacy groups pushes for new legislation and programmes to support young people in historically marginalized groups, opposes policies perceived as harmful for these children, and pursues more equal distribution of resources (material and financial) among young people. This work will have a much deeper impact the closer and clearer its link to changing the pedagogical core to liberate learning. Crafting, testing, and refining over time their theories of action to link their key strategies to improved teaching and learning (see Chapter 4) will only enhance the reach and depth of the important work advanced by advocacy groups.

In most people's minds, politics and teacher unions are almost inseparable concepts. Many factors place teachers' unions in a unique position to advance the renewal of public education. These include their collective power and institutional leverage to negotiate fair compensation and adequate working conditions for teachers, their unique position as vehicles to communicate teachers' concerns to policymakers, their capacity to support teacher professional learning and educational innovation, and their ability to facilitate strong relationships within educational systems.

This being said, liberating learning across entire educational system requires a new logic in the relationship between governments and unions. In this new logic:

1. students are placed at the centre;
2. unions and governments prioritize the advancement of a shared learning agenda;
3. a culture of transparency and trust is intentionally nurtured;
4. politics is embraced as part of the work;
5. conditions and incentives are created to trigger and grow the intrinsic motivation of adults in the system to liberate learning; and
6. adequate compensation and working conditions for teachers and staff are secured.

Some teacher unions are already advancing agendas of this kind. And there is a growing body of evidence that brings greater clarity to the specific ways in which teacher unions can and do help galvanize and support the type of movements that will be required to reinvent public education.

A lot of rhetoric portrays teacher unions as major obstacles to education reform, calling for their elimination or the undermining of their political power. However, the evidence to sustain this position is remarkably weak. For one thing, when state and national systems have taken steps to weaken the influence of their unions, educational outcomes don't change or get worse. On the contrary, a growing body of evidence demonstrates that unions can play a fundamental role in enhancing student learning, strengthening the teaching profession, and developing coherence in educational systems.[6] For starters, virtually every top performing education system you can think of has strong teacher unions. Finland? Checked. Canada? Checked. Japan? Checked.[7]

Teacher unions have historically played roles that are crucial for well-functioning education systems. One such role is ensuring fair remuneration and reasonable working conditions for teachers. Teacher working conditions have a direct impact on the quality of teaching and on teachers' sense of fulfilment and satisfaction, as well as on the role these play in attracting – or discouraging – talented candidates to pursue a career in education. Another primary function of unions is to help bring teachers' concerns to the attention of policymakers. This is an especially important role in a sector where teachers have little to no formal authority to discuss, shape, or design education policy, and where policymakers are too far removed from the realities of educational practice.

Beyond these legally delineated, labour-related roles, some unions are playing other roles that are beneficial to public education as a whole. These roles include facilitating the development of new policy ideas, encouraging educational experimentation and innovation, supporting the professional learning and career development of teachers, and nurturing teacher leadership (Bascia & Osmond, 2013; Bascia, 2009).

More recent research reveals the strong impact that partnerships between unions and management can have on improving student outcomes and nurturing cultures of collaboration in schools and across entire educational systems. Over the past seven years, Saul Rubinstein and John McCarthy have conducted a series of studies to examine the relationship between the quality of union–management partnerships in districts, patterns of collaboration within schools, and student achievement (Rubinstein & McCarthy, 2012, 2014, 2016; McCarthy & Rubinstein, 2017).[8] Union–management partnerships are defined as "institutional arrangements that provide opportunities for union leaders, administrators, and teachers to work together identifying and solving problems, planning, and making decisions" (Rubinstein & McCarthy, 2016, p. 1115). Their findings are worth noting.

First, the strength of a union–management partnership in a school has a positive and significant effect on the frequency and quality of teacher collaboration and on student achievement, both in plain achievement scores and in rates of improvement in performance from one year to the next (Rubinstein & McCarthy, 2014). Second, these positive effects hold even after controlling for poverty (measured as the percentage of students eligible for free and reduced lunches). This means that in schools serving students in similar socio-economic circumstances, schools with stronger union–management partnerships have more robust internal collaboration, better student outcomes, and higher rates of improvement in student outcomes from one year to the next than schools with weaker partnerships (Rubinstein & McCarthy, 2016). [9] Third, stronger union–management partnerships at the district level are related to stronger teacher collaboration within schools in a district. Furthermore, stronger union–management partnerships are associated with more frequent informal communication between principals and union representatives, lower teacher turnover, stronger commitment of teachers to the school especially in high poverty schools, more frequent connection with other schools, and a stronger sense among school-based union leaders of their role in supporting teacher collaboration in schools (McCarthy & Rubinstein, 2017).

Grounded in these findings, the causal pathway between union–management partnerships, teacher collaboration, and student achievement, can be outlined as follows. Strong union–management partnerships enable more extensive communication and collaboration among teachers within the school, as well as more frequent and informal communication between union representatives and principals. Teacher collaboration within the school, in turn, has a stronger effect on student outcomes the more it is focused on a) analysing evidence of student learning to improve pedagogical practice; b) developing coherence across grades, subjects, and the curriculum; and c) developing an environment of trust, a shared direction, and mutual support.

Look at the role played by unions in these partnerships through a social movement lens and their importance to liberating learning becomes even more evident. Unions can be powerful vehicles for strategic capacity. As defined earlier, strategic capacity is the capacity to turn what you have into what you need to get what you want. Social movements have winning chances over their opponents when they have stronger motivation, better access to salient knowledge, and better learning processes. As advocates for the wellbeing of educators, teacher unions are uniquely positioned to create working conditions that nurture their intrinsic motivation to liberate learning. As brokers between ministries of education and teachers, they have unparalleled access to salient knowledge that can help advance the cause of liberating learning. And the more they turn their spaces of deliberation with teachers into opportunities for continuous learning in the service of widespread pedagogical change, the more potent their role will be in liberating learning across entire educational systems.

Notes

1 A good account of teachers' protests in the United States and Latin America over education reforms seen as threatening teachers' working conditions or public education as a whole can be found in *Educational Courage* (Schniedewind & Shapon-Shevin, 2012); *Despite the Odds* (Grindle, 2004), and in *The Politics of Policies* (Stein, Tomassi, Echebarría, Lora, & Payne, 2005). Grossman (2010) offers a good analysis of how a network of progressive educators in the United States operated as a social movement to obtain a waiver from mandatory tests for their high school students, using instead student portfolios to assess student performance. Finally, Salinas and Fraser (2011) examine the student-led social movements in Chile that emerged in opposition to inadequate and unequal access to educational opportunity in the country.

2 In social physics (Pentland, 2014), this is described as the combination of *engagement* – focused, cooperative interaction within a particular network – and *exploration* – searching for new, potentially valuable ideas and practices through links with people or organizations outside the network. Effective networks do both.

3 Before embarking in open political confrontation, movements of pedagogical renewal can deliberate collectively around questions such as the following: In what ways can we use the new policy or programme to our advantage? Is open political confrontation the best use of our resources? Can we organize for political confrontation while sustaining our work to liberate learning on the ground?

4 I have to confess this is taken almost literally from Episode VIII in *Star Wars: The Last Jedi*. When rebel pilot Rose saves Finn (former storm trooper turned into rebel hero) in the last second as he heads straight to the massive cannon from the galactic empire that is about to shoot and destroy the base where the last few rebels in the galaxy are hiding, she tells him the Resistance will win "Not by fighting what we hate, but saving what we love."

5 In the case of Mexico, the National Revolutionary Party (PRI for its initials in Spanish) took the presidency back in 2012, after 12 years of ruling of the conservative party (Partido Acción Nacional, or PAN). As often happens with political transitions in many countries, the new government sought to remove as much of the legacy of the prior government as possible, and this included PEMLE/EIMLE. One year after, leaders of PEMLE were asked to leave the Ministry. The Tutorial Networks now continue through the work of a small non-governmental organization (Redes de Tutoría/Aprender con Interés), and the National Council for the Promotion of Education (CONAFE), which is now spreading tutorial networks to over 30,000 schools in small rural communities across Mexico. In Colombia, the decentralization of the Ministry of Education in the early 1990s pulled most of the energy of the departments (the equivalent of Provinces or States) and its municipalities into figuring out how to take on their new responsibilities, considerably deviating their attention and support to Escuela Nueva. Decentralization also made it practically impossible for the small central leadership team to manage the program in the new system. While in a centralized system the leadership of Escuela Nueva had to simply interact with teams from the 32 departments in the country, in the new decentralized system, they had to negotiate individually with over 1,000 municipalities. Being aware of the impossibility of continuing to operate within the educational bureaucracy, the leadership of Escuela Nueva decided to leave the Ministry and re-organize as a non-governmental organization.

6 See for example Bascia and Osmond (2013); Bascia (2009); Campbell et al. (2016); Hargreaves et al. (2009); Rubinstein and McCarthy (2012, 2014, 2016).

7 Notice I said that unions *can* play a fundamental role in the renewal of educational systems. They don't always do. Many unions maintain industrial thinking as their dominant mindset to ponder their options, design their strategies, and carry on their actions. At best, this limits the reach and depth of their impact on educational systems. At worst, it might get in the way of system improvements that are beneficial to both students and teachers. This being said, the fact remains that virtually every top performing educational system has a strong union.

8 The first study (Rubinstein & McCarthy, 2012) was a qualitative, cross-district study that looked at how six high-performing districts with strong union–management partnerships (in California, Florida, Virginia, New York, Minnesota, and Ohio) were supporting cultures of collaboration in schools centred on enhancing teaching quality and student achievement. The second (Rubinstein & McCarthy, 2014) was a quantitative study to measure the relationship between quality of union–management partnerships, the patterns of teacher collaboration schools, and student achievement. This study focused on a single school district (ABC Unified in California) and looked more closely at the density and nature of communication between teachers in schools. Within school collaboration was measured as the frequency of communication between teachers in regards to four major areas: review of student performance data; curricular, cross-grade and cross-subject integration; advising and learning about instructional practice; and giving and receiving mentoring. The third study (Rubinstein & McCarthy, 2016), also quantitative in nature, and also focused on the ABC Unified school district, examined the relationship between the strength of union–management partnerships in a school and student outcomes, as well as the mediating effects of the strength of collaboration within a school. In this case, "collaboration" was merely measured as the perceived level of meaningfulness and collaboration in the development of the school improvement plan and the initiatives undertaken by the

school. A fourth study (McCarthy & Rubinstein, 2017) examines the relationship between the strength of union–management partnerships in school and teacher commitment, within-school collaboration, and connections with other schools.

9 More specifically, Rubinstein and McCarthy (2014) found that: 1) *Students do better when they attend schools with stronger partnerships.* Stronger union–management partnerships are associated with higher API scores and higher API improvement from one year to the next, after controlling for poverty; 2) *In schools with stronger union–management partnerships there is significantly denser collaboration between teachers* around the following four areas: student-performance data; curriculum development and cross-subject and cross-grade integration; advising and learning about pedagogical practices; and giving or receiving mentoring. Schools with highest levels of partnership have on average twice the internal communication density than schools with the lowest levels of partnership; 3) *Collaboration focused on the four areas mentioned in the point above is associated with higher API performance scores and greater improvement in scores from one year to the next*; 4) *The effect of union–management partnerships in a school on student outcomes is mediated by the strength of collaboration within the school.* The measure used to calculate the strength of union–management partnerships is the average rating of such strength estimated by the district superintendent and union representatives in schools, while the strength of collaboration within the school is measured as the perceived degree of meaningfulness and collaborative nature of the school improvement plan and the school initiatives; and 5) *Stronger union–management partnerships are associated with stronger communication between principals and union representatives.*

7

ROLLING UP OUR SLEEVES

These are exciting times for education and daunting times for humanity. The amazing technological developments of the past few decades allow vast numbers of people to access massive amounts of knowledge in mere seconds, connect with people all over the world, and collectively tackle problems once considered unsolvable. At the same time, never before has humanity and the planet been so close to the precipice. One thing is certain. Maintaining the status quo in schools and school systems will only get us closer to it. I for one am not sure that even our best collective efforts will be powerful enough to reverse our path towards the precipice. And yet, I believe that the cause of liberating learning is worth our best efforts. As revolutionary thinker Antonio Gramsci would put it, in times like these we have to act with the pessimism of the intellect and the optimism of the will.

In this book, I have laid down a basic set of principles of action to liberate learning in classrooms, schools, and entire school systems. I have used the concept of social movements as a metaphor for a new paradigm to think about and pursue educational change. I believe this new paradigm has a good chance to take us closer to the goal of turning schools and school systems into vibrant places for learning and living examples of the democratic societies we aspire to become; into places where our younger generations practise, in the present, what it means to be confident learners and active, compassionate citizens. I have argued that the challenge of fundamentally changing the logic of schooling is not so much a technical matter as it is a cultural and political project. Social movements have served as the most powerful collective agents of cultural renewal throughout history. In their ways of operating lie important clues to radically redefine how young people and adults interact with each other in schools, and how administrators and educators interact with each other in educational systems.

The cultural change advocated for throughout this book is at odds with what we have come to take for granted in schools and school systems about what it means to learn, to teach, and to do education policy. And yet, its effectiveness and chances for success lie in its compatibility with our human condition. Advancing educational change as a social movement links us to our hard-wired inclination and capacity to learn, with our need to engage in work that is intrinsically motivating, to continuously get better, to connect with others, and to pursue a purpose larger than ourselves.

As my mentor Gabriel Cámara once said, military interventions – as conventional school reform – are very expensive, but revolutions are free. The feasibility of widespread pedagogical change proposed here lies on its reliance on a resource that each one of us has access to, a resource that Ivan Illich argued is the single resource that is equally distributed among fellow humans. Such resource is our capacity to act. We have come to organize classrooms, schools, and school systems in ways that limit how our capacity to act can be mobilized. As a result, we have created institutions that induce scarcity: scarcity of time to engage in deep and meaningful conversations with young people and adults, scarcity of space and time to work collaboratively in tackling unsolved problems, scarcity of opportunities to collectively identify and change what gets in the way of powerful learning. Once our capacity to act is unleashed and put to work towards a common cause – liberating learning – and once it reaches a critical mass, it will be hard to stop.

These are times when everyone seems extremely busy, always having something else to do, prioritizing what's urgent over what's important. And this constant distraction has moved us away from the full realization of our humanity. Humanity at its best comes to the surface when we find deep purpose in what we do, when we get better at it, when we connect with others, and when we have some freedom to decide what to do, when, how, or with whom. Bringing our attention back to what really matters in education – nurturing relationships that liberate learning – can unleash powerful energy for the much-needed changes in our schools and school systems. It can bring us closer to the fulfilment of our shared humanity. And it makes it more likely that our children and youth will have a fighting chance to survive, thrive in, and positively change the messy world they're inheriting from us.

In the pursuit of liberating learning, you will likely encounter important roadblocks, closed alleys, and perhaps vicious attacks from people and organizations with a vested interest in maintaining the status quo. But one of the most powerful deterrents lies within ourselves. To explain this point, I'll use one of my favourite movie scenes.

V for Vendetta is the story of an underground vigilante known as V (Hugo Weaving) who pursues justice in a post-war London ruled by an authoritarian, fascist regime. V befriends a young journalist called Evey (Natalie Portman), who becomes an ally in his fight against the oppressive regime. At one point in the story. Evey is captured and put in prison, where she undergoes physical and psychological torture. She spends several weeks in a small cell, the door of which has a small window with vertical bars. The small window is her only space available to see outside, towards the hallway. Every time she looks out the window, she sees a guard standing in the hallway.

Upon having an experience of personal enlightenment, Evey heads to the door of her cell and pushes it. To her surprise, the door opens – it had never been locked! She sticks her head out the door and sees the guard in the hallway, so she rushes back in. She looks out again several times and notices the guard is not moving. She gets the courage to step out of her cell and starts walking down the hall. The guard continues motionless. When she finally walks by the guard, she realizes it's a mannequin. The real constraint to Evey's freedom was her perception of the barriers that stood in her way.

There are many concrete barriers to our capacity to act. But some – and perhaps many – of the most important ones lie in our perceptions of what is possible, what's allowed, and what the consequences of our actions will be. Metaphorically speaking, we all live, in one way or another, in cells like the one that kept Evey prisoner. I invite you to push the door of your cell and, if it opens, take a walk down the hall.

The next decade or two might be the definitive time to see whether there is any bright future in sight for educational systems around the world. It's time to roll up our sleeves!

REFERENCES

Alberoni, F. (1984). *Movement and Institution*. New York, NY: Columbia University Press.

Apple, M. (2004). *Ideology and Curriculum*. 3rd edn. London: Routledge.

Argyris, C., & Schön, D. (1978). *Organizational Learning: A Theory of Action Perspective*. Reading, MA: Addison-Wesley.

Bascia, N. (2009). "Pushing on the Paradigm: Research on Teachers' Organizations as Policy Actors". In G. Sykes, B. Schneider, & D. Plank (Eds) *Handbook of Educational Policy Research*. (pp. 785–792). New York, NY: Routledge, American Educational Research Association.

Bascia, N., & Osmond, P. (2013). *Teacher Union Governmental Relations in the Context of Educational Reform*. Brussels, Belgium: Education International.

Bascia, N., & Rottman, C. (2011). "What's So Important About Teachers' Working Conditions?: The Fatal Flaw in North American Educational Reform". *Journal of Education Policy*, 26(6). doi:10.1080/02680939.2010.543156

Bellanca, J.A. (2015). *Deeper Learning: Beyond 21st Century Skills*. Bloomington, IN: Solution Tree.

Berman, P. (1981). "Educational Change: An Implementation Paradigm". In R. Lehming & M. Kane (Eds) *Improving Schools: Using What We Know*. (pp. 253–286). Beverly Hills, CA: Sage Publications.

Bernstein, B. (1977). "Social Class, Language, and Socialization". In J. Karabel & A.H. Halsey (Eds) *Power and Ideology in Education*. (pp. 473–486). New York, NY: Oxford University Press.

Blankstein, A.M., Noguera, P., & Kelly, L. (2016). *Excellence through Equity: Five Principles of Courageous Leadership to Guide Achievement for Every Student*. Alexandria, VA: ASCD Books.

Bourdieu, P. (1974). "School as a Conservative Force: Scholastic and Cultural Inequalities". In L. Eggleston (Ed.) *Contemporary Research in the Sociology of Education*. (pp. 32–46). London: Methuen.

Bourdieu, P., & Passeron, J-C. (1977). *Reproduction in Education, Society, and Culture*. London, UK: Sage.

Brandon, J., Hanna, P., & Negropontes, D. (2015). *Superintendents Who Lead Learning: Lessons from Six Highly Successful School Jurisdictions*. Calgary, AB: University of Calgary/College of Alberta School Superintendents.

Broccoli, A. (1979). *Antonio Gramsci y la Educación como Hegemonía*. Mexico: Nueva Imagen.

Bruner, J. (1986). "Two Modes of Thought". In *Actual Minds, Possible Worlds*. Cambridge, MA: Harvard University Press.

Bryk, A., Gomez, L., Grunow, A., & LeMahieu, P. (2015). *Learning to Improve: How America's Schools Can Get Better at Getting Better*. Cambridge, MA: Harvard Education Press.

Cámara, G. (2008). *Otra Educación Básica es Posible*. Mexico: Siglo XXI.

Campbell, C., Lieberman, A., Yashkina, A., Rodway, J., Alexander, S., & Malik, S. (2016). Teacher Learning and Leadership Program. Research Report for 2015–2016. Toronto, ON: Ontario Teachers' Federation.

Chenoweth, K. (2007). *It's Being Done: Academic Success in Unexpected Schools*. Cambridge, MA: Harvard Education Press.

Chenoweth, K. (2009). *How It's Being Done: Urgent Lessons from Unexpected Schools*. Cambridge, MA: Harvard Education Press.

City, E.A., Elmore, R.F., Fiarman, S.E., & Teitel, L. (2009). *Instructional Rounds: A Network Approach to Improving Teaching and Learning*. Cambridge, MA: Harvard Education Press.

Cohen, D.K., Raudenbush, S., & Ball, D.L. (2003). "Resources, Instruction, and Research". *Educational Evaluation and Policy Analysis*, 25, 119–142. doi:10.3102/01623737025002119

Colbert, V., & Arboleda, J. (2016). "Bringing a Student-Centred Participatory Pedagogy to Scale in Colombia". *Journal of Educational Change*, 17, 385–410. doi:10.1007/s10833-10016-9283-9287

Csikszentmihalyi, M. (1990). *Flow: The Psychology of Optimal Experience*. New York, NY: Harper Collins.

Cuban, L. (1984). *How Teachers Taught: Constancy and Change in American Classrooms (1890–1980)*. New York, NY: Longman.

Cybulski, T.G., Hoy, W.K., & Sweetland, S.R. (2005). "The Roles of Collective Efficacy on Teachers and Fiscal Efficiency in Student Achievement". *Journal of Educational Administration*, 43(5), 439–461.

Daly, A.J. (Ed.) (2010). *Social Network Theory and Educational Change*. Cambridge, MA: Harvard Education Press.

Darling-Hammond, L., & Sykes, G. (Eds) (1999). *Teaching as the Learning Profession. Handbook of Policy and Practice*. San Francisco, CA: Jossey-Bass.

Datnow, A. & Park, V. (2009). "Conceptualizing Implementation: Large-Scale Reform in an Era of Complexity". In G. Sykes & D. Plank (Eds) *AERA Handbook on Educational Policy Research* (pp. 348–361). Washington, DC: American Educational Research Association.

Deci, E.L. (1996). *Why We Do What We Do: Understanding Self-Motivation*. New York, NY: Penguin Books.

Deci, E.L., & Ryan, R.M. (1980). "The Empirical Exploration of Intrinsic Motivational Processes". In L. Berkowitz (Ed.) *Advances in Experimental Social Psychology*. Vol. 13 (pp. 39–80). New York, NY: Academic Press.

Dewey, J. (1938). *Experience and Education*. New York, NY: Kappa Delta Pi.

DiMaggio, P. (1997). "Culture and Cognition". *Annual Review of Sociology*, 23, 263–287.

Doidge, N. (2007). *The Brain that Changes Itself: Stories of Personal Triumph from the Frontiers of Brain Science*. New York, NY: Penguin Books.

Donohoo, J. (2016). *Collective Efficacy: How Educators' Beliefs Impact Student Learning.* Thousand Oaks, CA: Corwin.

Doyle, W. (1983). "Academic Work". *Review of Educational Research*, 53(2), 159–199.

Duncan-Andrade, J.M. & Morrell, E. (2008). *The Art of Critical Pedagogy: Possibilities for Moving from Theory to Practice in Urban Schools.* New York, NY: Peter Lang Publishing.

Earl, L., & Katz, S. (2005). *What Makes a Network a Learning Network?* Nottingham, UK: National College for School Leadership.

Eells, R.J. (2011). Meta-Analysis of the Relationship between Collective Teacher Efficacy and Student Achievement. Doctoral dissertation. Chicago, IL: Loyola University of Chicago.

Elmore, R.F. (1996). "Getting to Scale with Good Educational Practice". *Harvard Educational Review*, 66(1), 1–26.

Elmore, R.F. (2004). *School Reform from the Inside Out: Policy, Practice, and Performance.* Cambridge, MA: Harvard Education Press.

Elmore, R.F. (2016). "Reflections on the Role of Tutoría in the Future of Learning". Available at: https://redesdetutoria.com/download/reflections-on-the-role-of-tutoria -in-the-future-of-learning/

Elmore, R.F., Peterson, P.L., & McCarthey, S.J. (1996). *Restructuring in the Classroom: Teaching, Learning and School Organization.* San Francisco, CA: Jossey-Bass.

Evans, R. (1996). "The Culture of Resistance". In *The Human Side of Change.* (pp. 40–50). San Francisco, CA: Jossey-Bass.

Farrell, J., Manion, C., & Rincón-Gallardo, S. (2017). "Reinventing Schooling: Successful Radical Alternatives from the Global South". In K. Bickmore, R. Hayhoe, C. Manion, K. Mundy, & R. Read (Eds) *Comparative and International Education: Issues for Teachers.* 2nd edition (pp. 59–87). Toronto/Vancouver: Canadian Scholars.

Faure, E., Herrera, F., Kaddoura, A-R., Lopes, H., Petrovsky, A.V., Rahnema, M., & Champion Ward, F. (1972). *Learning to Be: The World of Education Today and Tomorrow.* Paris, France: UNESCO.

Fielding, M. (2001). "Students as Radical Change Agents". *Journal of Educational Change*, 2(2), 123–141. doi:10.1023/A:1017949213447

Fine, S. (2017). "Why Dewey Needs Freire and Vice-versa: A Call for Critical Deeper Learning". Learning Deeply Blog, *Education Week*. Available at http://blogs.edweek. org/edweek/learning_deeply/2016/11/why_dewey_needs_freire_and_vice_versa_a_ca ll_for_critical_deeper_learning.html Accessed 24 November 2017.

Ford, M. (2016). *Rise of the Robots: Technology and the Threat of a Jobless Future.* New York, NY: Basic Books.

Freire, P. (1970). *Pedagogy of the Oppressed.* New York, NY: The Continuum International Publishing Group.

Fullan, M. (1991). *The Meaning of Educational Change.* New York, NY: Teachers College Press.

Fullan, M. (2011). Choosing the Wrong Drivers for Whole System Reform. Seminar Series Paper No. 204. Victoria, AU: Centre for Strategic Education.

Fullan, M. (2014). *The Principal: Three Keys to Maximizing Impact.* San Francisco, CA: Jossey-Bass.

Fullan, M. (2015). *Freedom to Change: Four Strategies to Put your Inner Drive into Overdrive.* San Francisco, CA: Jossey-Bass.

Fullan, M. (2015a). "Leadership from the Middle: A System Strategy". Canadian Education Association, December 2015, pp. 22–26.

Fullan, M. (2018). *Nuance: Why Some Leaders Succeed while Others Fail.* Thousand Oaks, CA: Corwin.

Fullan, M., & Hargreaves, A. (2016). *Bringing the Profession Back In: A Call to Action.* Oxford, OH: Learning Forward.

Fullan, M., Hill, P., & Rincón-Gallardo, S. (2017). Deep Learning: Shaking the Foundations. Deep Learning Series. Issue 3. Toronto, ON: New Pedagogies for Deep Learning. Available at: http://npdl.global/wp-content/uploads/2017/03/npdl-case_study_3.pdf

Fullan, M., & Quinn, J. (2015). *Coherence: The Right Drivers in Action in Schools, Districts, and Systems.* Thousand Oaks, CA: Corwin.

Fullan, M., Quinn, J., & McEachen, J. (2017). *Deep Learning: Engage the World, Change the World.* Thousand Oaks, CA: Corwin.

Fullan, M., Rincón-Gallardo, S., & Watson, N. (2016). California's Golden Opportunity: District Case Studies of Professional Capital. Toronto, ON: Motion Leadership. Available at: https://michaelfullan.ca/californias-golden-opportunity/

Fullan, M., Rodway, J., & Rincón-Gallardo, S. (2016). New Pedagogies for Deep Learning. Toward District Wide Deep Learning: A Cross Case Study. Deep Learning Series, Issue 2. Toronto, ON: NPDL. Available at: http://npdl.global/wp-content/uploads/2017/01/npdl-case_study_1.pdf

Gallagher, M.J., Malloy, J., & Ryerson, R. (2016). "Achieving Excellence: Bringing Effective Literacy Pedagogy to Scale in Ontario's Publicly-Funded Education System". *Journal of Educational Change*, 17, 477–504.

Ganz, M. (2009). *Why David Sometimes Wins: Leadership, Organization, and Strategy in the California Farm Worker Movement.* New York, NY: Oxford University Press.

Ganz, M. (2010). "Leading Change: Leadership, Organization, and Social Movements". In N. Nohria, & R. Khurana (Eds) *Handbook of Leadership Theory and Practice: A Harvard Business School Centennial Colloquium.* Chapter 19 (pp. 527–568). Boston, MA: Harvard Business Press.

Garcia-Huidobro, J.C., Nannemann, A., Bacon, C., & Thompson, K. (2017). "Evolution in Educational Change: A Literature Review of the Historical Core of the Journal of Educational Change". *Journal of Educational Change*, 18(3), 263–293.

Gaskell, J. (2004). "Educational Change and the Women's Movement: Lessons from British Columbia Schools in the 1970s". *Educational Policy*, 18(2), 291–310.

Gaskell, J. (2008). "Learning from the Women's Movement about Educational Change". *Discourse: Studies in the Cultural Politics of Education*, 29(4), 437–449.

Gatto, J.T. (1992). *Dumbing Us Down: The Hidden Curriculum of American Schools.* British Columbia, Canada: New Society Publishers.

Gatto, J.T. (2009). *Weapons of Mass Instruction: A Schoolteacher's Journey through the Dark World of Compulsory Schooling.* British Columbia, Canada: New Society Publishers.

Ginwright, S., & James, T. (2002). "From Assets to Agents of Change: Social Justice, Organizing, and Youth Development". *New Directions for Youth Development*, 96, 27–46.

Giroux, H.A. (1983). *Theory and Resistance in Education: A Pedagogy for the Opposition.* South Hadley, MA: Bergin & Garvey Publishers.

Gladwell, M. (2008). *Outliers: The Story of Success.* New York, NY: Little, Brown, and Company.

Glennan, T.K., Bodilly, S.J., Galegher, J.R., & Kerr, K.A. (2004). *Expanding the Reach of Education Reforms: Perspectives from Leaders in the Scale-Up of Educational Interventions.* Santa Monica, CA: RAND.

Goddard, R.D. (1998). The Effects of Collective Teacher Efficacy on Student Achievement in Urban Public Elementary Schools. Doctoral Dissertation. Retrieved from http://etd.ohiolink.edu/

Goddard, R.D. (2001). "Collective Efficacy: A Neglected Construct in the Study of Schools and Student Achievement". *Journal of Educational Psychology*, 93(3), 467–476.

Goddard, R.D., Hoy, W.K., & Woolfolk Hoy, A. (2000). "Collective Teacher Efficacy: Its Meaning, Measure, and Impact on Student Achievement". *American Educational Research Journal*, 37(2), 479–507.

Goddard, R.D., LoGerfo, L., & Hoy, W. (2004). "High School Accountability: The Role of Perceived Collective Efficacy". *Educational Policy*, 18(3), 403–425.

Gramsci, A. (1971). *Selections from the Prison Notebooks*. New York, NY: International Publishers.

Granovetter, M. (1973). "The Strength of Weak Ties". *American Journal of Sociology*, 78, 1360–1380.

Grindle, M.S. (2004). *Despite the Odds. The Contentious Politics of Education Reform*. Princeton, NJ: Princeton University Press.

Grossman, F. (2010). "Dissent From Within: How Educational Insiders Use Protest to Create Policy Change". *Educational Policy*, 24(4), 655–686.

Hargreaves, A., & Ainscow, M. (2015). "The Top and Bottom of Leadership and Change". *Phi Delta Kappan*, 97(3), 42–48.

Hargreaves, A., & Braun, H. (2012). Leading for All: A Research Report of the Development, Design, Implementation and Impact of Ontario's "Essential for Some, Good for All" Initiative. Ontario, Canada: Council of Ontario Directors of Education.

Hargreaves, A., Crocker, R., Davis, B., McEwen, L., Sahlberg, P., Shirley, D., & Sumara, D. (2009). The Learning Mosaic: A Multiple Perspectives Review of the Alberta Initiative for School Improvement. Edmonton, AB: Alberta Education.

Hargreaves, A., & Fink, D. (2006). *Sustainable Leadership*. San Francisco, CA: Jossey-Bass.

Hargreaves, A., & Fullan, M. (2012). *Professional Capital: Transforming Teaching in Every School*. New York/Toronto: Teachers College Press/Ontario Principal's Council.

Hargreaves, A., & O'Connor, M. (2018). *Collaborative Professionalism: When Teaching Together Means Learning for All*. Thousand Oaks, CA: Corwin.

Hargreaves, A., & Shirley, D. (2012). *The Global Fourth Way: The Quest for Educational Excellence*. Thousand Oaks, CA: Corwin.

Hattie, J. (2009). *Visible Learning: A Synthesis of Over 800 Meta-Analyses Relating to Achievement*. New York, NY: Routledge.

Hawkins, D. (1974). "I, Thou, and It". In *The Informed Vision: Essays on Learning and Human Nature*. (pp. 49–62). New York, NY: Agathon Books.

Hoffman, N. (2015). *Let's Get Real: Deeper Learning and the Power of the Workplace*. Students at the Centre: Deeper Learning Research Series. Boston, MA: Jobs for the Future.

Holt, J. (1977). *Instead of Education: Ways to Help People Do Things Better*. New York, NY: Delacorte Press.

hooks, b. (1994). *Teaching to Transgress: Education as the Practice of Freedom*. New York, NY: Routledge.

Hoy, Anita W., & Davis, H.A. (2006). "Teacher Self-Efficacy and its Influence on the Achievement of Adolescents". In F. Pajares & T. Urdan, *Self-Efficacy Beliefs of Adolescents*. (pp. 117–137). Greenwich, CT: Information Age Publishing.

Illich, I. (1970). *Deschooling Society*. New York, NY: Marion Boyars Publishers.

Jenkins, L. (2012). "Reversing the Downslide of Student Enthusiasm". *School Administrator*, 5(69), 16–17. Available at: www.aasa.org/content.aspx?id=23242

Johnson, S.M. et al. (2015). *Achieving Coherence in District Reform: Managing the Relationship Between the Central Office and Schools*. Cambridge, MA: Harvard Education Press.

Kane, L. (2000). "Popular Education and the Landless People's Movement in Brazil". *Studies in the Education of Adults*, 32(1), 36–50.

Katz, S., & Dack, L.A. (2012). *Intentional Interruption: Breaking Down Learning Barriers to Transform Professional Practice*. Thousand Oaks, CA: Corwin.

Kim, K.H. (2011). "The Creativity Crisis: The Decrease in Creative Thinking Scores on the Torrance Tests of Creative Thinking". *Creativity Research Journal*, 23(4), 285–295.

Kirshner, B. (2015). *Youth Activism in an Era of Education Inequality*. New York, NY: New York University Press.

Kuhn, T.S. (1970). *The Structure of Scientific Revolutions*. Chicago, IL: University of Chicago Press.

Latham, B., Lenz, B., & Ark, T.V. (2016). Preparing Students for a Project-Based World. Novato, CA: Getting Smart/Buck Institute for Education.

Leadbeater, C. (2012). *Innovation in Education: Lessons from Pioneers Around the World*. Qatar: Bloomsbury Qatar Foundation Publishing.

Leithwood, K. (2006). *Teaching Working Conditions that Matter: Evidence for Change*. Toronto, ON: Teachers' Federation of Ontario.

Leithwood, K., Seashore-Louis, K., Anderson, S., & Wahlstrom, K. (2004). How Leadership Influences Student Learning: A Review of Research for the Learning from Leadership Project. New York, NY: The Wallace Foundation.

Lemov, D., Woolway, E., & Yezzi, K. (2012). *Practice Perfect: 42 Rules for Getting Better at Getting Better*. San Francisco, CA: Jossey-Bass.

Lepper, M.R., Corpus, J.H., & Iyengar, S.S. (2005). "Intrinsic and Extrinsic Motivational Orientations in the Classroom: Age Differences and Academic Correlates". *Journal of Educational Psychology*, 97(2), 184–196. doi:10.1037/0022-0663.97.2.184

Little, J.W. (1982). "Norms of Collegiality and Experimentation: Workplace Conditions of School Success". *American Educational Research Journal*, 19(3), 325–340.

Llewellyn, G. (1998). *The Teenage Liberation Handbook: How to Quit School and Get a Real Life and Education*. Revised edn. Eugene, OR: Lowry House.

MacNamara, B.N., Hambrick, D.Z., & Oswald, F.L. (2014). "Deliberate Practice and Performance in Music, Games, Sports, Education, and Professions: A Meta-Analysis". *Psychological Science*, 25(8), 1608–1618. doi:10.1177/0956797614535810

Makary, M.A., & Daniel, M. (2016). "Medical Error – the Third Leading Cause of Death in the US". *British Medical Journal*, *353*: i2139. doi:10.1136/bmj.i2139

McAdam, D., McCarthey, J.D., & Zald, M.N. (Eds) (1996). *Comparative Perspectives on Social Movements: Political Opportunities, Mobilizing Structures, and Cultural Framings*. Cambridge, UK: Cambridge University Press.

McCarthy, J.E., & Rubinstein, S.A. (2017). National Study on Union-Management Partnerships and Educator Collaboration in US Public Schools. Working Paper. Collaborative School Leadership Initiative.

Mehta, J. (2013). *The Allure of Order: High Hopes, Dashed Expectations, and the Troubled Quest to Remake American Schooling*. New York, NY: Oxford University Press.

Mehta, J., & Fine, S. (2015). The Why, What, Where, and How of Deeper Learning in American Secondary Schools. Students at the Center: Deeper Learning Research Series. Boston, MA: Jobs for the Future.

Mehta, J., Schwartz, R.B., & Hess, F.M. (2012). *The Futures of School Reform*. Cambridge, MA: Harvard Education Press.

Meier, D. (2002). *The Power of Their Ideas: Lessons for America from a Small School in Harlem*. Boston, MA: Beacon Press.

Merzenich, M. (2013). *Soft-Wired: How the New Science of Brain Plasticity Can Change Your Life*. San Francisco, CA: Parnassus.

Mourshed, M., Chijioke, C., & Barber, M. (2010). *How the World's Most Improved School Systems Keep Getting Better*. London, UK: McKinsey & Company.

Nielsen, M. (2012). *Reinventing Discovery: The New Era of Networked Science*. Princeton, NJ: Princeton University Press.

Niesz, T., Korora, A., Burke Walkuski, C., & Foot, R. (2018). "Social Movements and Educational Research: Toward a United Field of Scholarship". *Teachers College Record*, 120(3).

Niesz, T., & Krishnamurthy, R. (2013). "Bureaucratic Activism and Radical School Change in Tamil Nadu, India". *Journal of Educational Change*, 14, 29–50.

Niesz, T., & Krishnamurthy, R. (2014). "Movement Actors in the Education Bureaucracy: The Figured World of Activity Based Learning in Tamil Nadu". *Anthropology & Education Quarterly*, 45(2), 148–166.

Niesz, T., & Ryan, K. (2018). "Teacher Ownership Versus Scaling Up System-Wide Educational Change: The Case of Activity Based Learning in South India". *Educational Research for Policy and Practice*. doi:10.1007/s10671–10018–9232–9238

Norton, A. (2004). *95 Theses on Politics, Culture, and Method*. New Haven, CT: Yale University Press.

Olson, K. (2009). *Wounded by School: Recapturing the Joy in Learning and Standing Up to Old School Culture*. New York, NY: Teachers College Press.

OECD (2011). Lessons from PISA for the United States. Strong Performers, Successful Reformers in Education. Paris, France: OECD.

OECD (2013). PISA 2012 Results: Excellence Through Equity: Giving Every Student the Chance to Succeed Volume II. Paris, France: OECD. doi:10.1787/9789264201132-en

Pentland, A. (2014). *Social Physics: How Good Ideas Spread*. New York, NY: Penguin.

Pink, D. (2006). *A Whole New Mind: Why Right Brainers Will Rule the Future*. New York, NY: Penguin.

Pink, D. (2009). *Drive: The Surprising Truth about What Motivates Us*. New York, NY: Riverhead Books.

Prensky, M. (2016). *Education to Better Their World: Unleashing the Power of 21st-Century Kids*. New York, NY: Teachers College Press.

Richardson, W. (2012). Why School? How Education Must Change When Learning and Information are Everywhere. TED Conferences.

Ries, E. (2017). *The Startup Way: How Modern Companies Use Entrepreneurial Management to Transform Culture and Drive Long-Term Growth*. New York, NY: Currency.

Rincón-Gallardo, S. (2016). "Large Scale Pedagogical Transformation as Widespread Cultural Change in Mexican Public Schools". *Journal of Educational Change*, 17, 411–436. doi:10.1007/s10833–10016–9286–9284

Rincón-Gallardo, S. (2017). Dewey and Freire Need Each Other to Fight a Common Enemy: Conventional Schooling. Blog post in *Education Week*'s Learning Deeply Blog. 26 July 2017. Available at: http://blogs.edweek.org/edweek/learning_deeply/2017/07/dewey_and_freire_need_each_other_to_fight_a_greater_enemy_conventional_schooling.html

Rincón-Gallardo, S. (2018). "In the Pursuit of Freedom and Social Justice: Four Theses to Reshape Educational Change". In H. Malone, S. Rincón-Gallardo, & K. Kew (Eds) *Future Directions of Educational Change: Social Justice, Professional Capital, and Systems Change* (pp. 17–33). London, UK: Routledge.

Rincón-Gallardo, S. & Elmore, R.F. (2012). "Transforming Teaching and Learning through Social Movement in Mexican Public Middle-Schools". *Harvard Educational Review*, 82(4), 471–490.

Rincón-Gallardo, S. & Fullan, M. (2016). "Essential Features of Effective Networks in Education". *Journal of Professional Capital and Community*, 1(1), 5–22.

Robinson, K., & Aronica, L. (2015). *Creative Schools: The Grassroots Revolution That's Transforming Education*. New York, NY: Penguin Books.

Robinson, V. (2011). *Student-Centred Leadership*. San Francisco, CA: Jossey-Bass.

Robinson, V., Lloyd, C.A., & Rowe, K.J. (2008). "The Impact of Leadership on Student Outcomes". *Education Administration Quarterly*, 44, 635–674.

Rochon, T.R. (1998). *Culture Moves: Ideas, Activism, and Changing Values*. Princeton, NJ: Princeton University Press.

Rogers, C.R. (1969). *Freedom to Learn*. Columbus, OH: Charles E. Merrill Publishing.

Rubinstein, S.A., & McCarty, J.E. (2012). "Public School Reform through Union-Management Collaboration". *Advances in Industrial and Labor Relations*, 20, 1–50.

Rubinstein, S.A., & McCarthy, J.E. (2014). *Teacher Unions and Management Partnerships: How Working Together Improves Student Achievement*. Washington, DC: Centre for American Progress.

Rubinstein, S.A., & McCarthy, J.E. (2016). "Union-Management Partnerships, Teacher Collaboration, and Student Performance". *ILR Review*, 69(5), 1114–1132.

Ryan, R.M., & Deci, E.L. (2000). "Self Determination Theory and the Facilitation of Intrinsic Motivation, Social Development, and Well-Being". *American Psychologist*, 55(1), 68–78.

Salinas, D., & Fraser, P. (2011). "Educational Opportunity and Contentious Politics: The 2011 Chilean Student Movement". *Berkeley Review of Education*, 3(1), 17–47.

Sarason, S. (1982). *The Culture of School and the Problem of Change*. Boston, MA: Allyn & Bacon.

Sarmiento, A., & Colbert, V. (2017). "Social Justice, Educational Change, and Escuela Nueva". In H.J. Malone, S. Rincón-Gallardo, & K. Kew (Eds) *Future Directions of Educational Change*. (pp. 53–70). New York, NY: Routledge.

Schiefelbein, E. (1993). In Search of the School of the 21st Century: Is Colombia's Escuela Nueva the Right Pathfinder? Santiago, Chile: UNESCO Regional Office for Latin America and the Caribbean.

Schniedewind, N., & Sapon-Shevin, M. (2012). *Educational Courage: Resisting the Ambush of Public Education*. Boston, MA: Beacon Press.

Schöning, M., & Witcomb, C. (2017). This is the One Skill your Child Needs for the Jobs of the Future. Available at https://www.weforum.org/agenda/2017/09/skills-children-need-work-future-play-lego. Accessed 23 November 2017.

Schwab, K. (2016). *The Fourth Industrial Revolution*. Geneva, Switzerland: World Economic Forum.

Scott, J.C. (1990). *Domination and the Arts of Resistance: Hidden Transcripts*. New Haven, CT: Yale University Press.

Scott, K. (2017). *Radical Candor: How to Be a Kick-Ass Boss without Losing Your Humanity*. New York, NY: St. Martin's Press.

Shalaby, C. (2017). *Troublemakers: Lessons in Freedom from Young People at School*. New York, NY: New York Press.

Siegel, D.J., & Payne Bryson, T. (2012). *The Whole-Brain Child: 12 Revolutionary Strategies to Nurture Your Child's Developing Mind*. New York, NY: Bantam Books.

Stein, E., Tommasi, M., Echebarría, K., Lora, E., & Payne, M. (Eds) (2005). *The Politics of Policies: Economic and Social Progress in Latin America*. Washington, DC: Interamerican Development Bank.

Stone, D., & Heen, S. (2014). *Thanks for the Feedback*. New York, NY: Viking.

Stoll, L.Bolam, R., McMahon, A., Wallace, M., & Thomas, S. (2006). "Professional Learning Communities: A Review of the Literature". *Journal of Educational Change*, 7, 221–258.

Tarrow, S. (2011). *Power in Movement: Social Movements and Contentious Politics*, 3rd edn. New York, NY: Cambridge University Press.

Thomas, P. (2009). *The Gramscian Moment: Philosophy, Hegemony and Marxism*. London, UK: Brill.

Thompson, D. (2015). A World without Work. *The Atlantic Daily*. Available at https://www. theatlantic.com/magazine/archive/2015/07/world-withoutwork/395294 Accessed 17 February 2017.

Torrance, E.P. (1968). "A Longitudinal Examination of the Fourth Grade Slump in Creativity". *Gifted Child Quarterly*, 12(4), 195–198.

Tucker, M. (2011). *Surpassing Shanghai: An Agenda for American Education Built on the World's Leading Systems*. Cambridge, MA: Harvard Education Press.

Tyack, D.B. (1974). *The One Best System: A History of American Urban Education*. Cambridge, MA: Harvard University Press.

van Horn Melton, J. (2003). *Absolutism and the Eighteenth-Century Origins of Compulsory Schooling in Prussia and Austria*. Cambridge, UK: Cambridge University Press.

Vygotsky, L.S. (1978). *Mind in Society: Development and Higher Psychological Processes*. Cambridge, MA: Harvard University Press.

Wagner, T., & Dintersmith, T. (2015). *Most Likely to Succeed: Preparing our Kids for the Innovation Era*. New York, NY: Simon and Schuster.

Willis, P. (1977). *Learning to Labour: How Working Class Kids Get Working Class Jobs*. Farnborough, UK: Saxon House.

Zaalouk, M. (2006). *The Pedagogy of Empowerment: Community Schools as a Social Movement in Egypt*. Cairo/New York: American University in Cairo Press.

Zavadsky, H. (2009). *Bringing School Reform to Scale: Five Award-Winning Urban Districts*. Cambridge, MA: Harvard Education Press.

INDEX